PERGAMON GENERAL PSYCHOLOGY SERIES

Editors: Arnold P. Goldstein, *Syracuse University*
Leonard Krasner, *SUNY, Stony Brook*

The Early Window:
Effects of Television on Children and Youth

PGPS-34

The Early Window:
Effects of Television on Children and Youth

ROBERT M. LIEBERT
JOHN M. NEALE

and

EMILY S. DAVIDSON

State University of New York at Stony Brook

PERGAMON PRESS INC.

New York · Toronto · Oxford · Sydney · Braunschweig

PERGAMON PRESS INC.
Maxwell House, Fairview Park, Elmsford, N.Y. 10523

PERGAMON OF CANADA LTD.
207 Queen's Quay West, Toronto 117, Ontario

PERGAMON PRESS LTD.
Headington Hill Hall, Oxford

PERGAMON PRESS (AUST.) PTY. LTD.
Rushcutters Bay, Sydney, N.S.W.

VIEWEG & SOHN GmbH
Burgplatz 1, Braunschweig

Copyright © 1973, Pergamon Press Inc.

Library of Congress Cataloging in Publication Data

Liebert, Robert M.   1942–
The early window.

(Pergamon general psychology series, 34)
1. Television and children. I. Neale, John M.,
1943–   joint author. II. Davidson, Emily S., 1948–
joint author. III. Title.
HQ784.T4L48   1973   301.16   72-8669
ISBN 0-08-017091-9
ISBN 0-08-017092-7 (pbk.)

ISBN 0-08-017780 8 (textbk. ed.)

Printed in the United States of America

710 042582-8

"... television can be considered to be a window on the world, a school if you will, through which the child first perceives his society and then learns from repeated example to cope with the vicissitudes of living."

John P. Murray, Ph.D.

Research Coordinator,
Surgeon General's Advisory
Committee on Television
And Social Behavior

CONTENTS

FOREWORD

Television for home viewers became a mass medium of communication in the United States in the years after the Second World War. Whereas by 1949 there were one million TV sets in American homes, two years later there were ten million, and by 1960 there were well over fifty million. By now, more American homes have television sets than any other electrical appliance; many more homes have TV than indoor plumbing.

Social scientists have been fascinated to watch this new medium ascend to stardom, elbowing other mass media from the center of the stage. Now, like aging actors, the other media are cast in supporting roles. Movies are produced in Hollywood not so much for the corner theater as for the TV screen. Big-circulation magazines like *Look*, *Life*, and *The Saturday Evening Post* have vanished from the American scene; today one of the two top-circulation magazines is *TV Guide*. Newspapers are now read, in part, because they comment on TV productions and list TV offerings; also they amplify and document the news the reader already knows from having seen it on TV. Radio is what you listen to while driving, when it would be unsafe to have your eyes on a TV set. Books gain huge readerships when their authors appear on TV talk shows.

Television has developed in our country as a commercial medium, with viewers paying for TV sets and for the electricity to keep them running, and with advertisers paying to put programs on the air. The split in costs is roughly fifty-fifty: what the American public spends in a year to buy sets is about matched by what advertisers spend to support broadcasting.

Members of the television industry think of their viewers as buyers. Their nomenclature is revealing. Whereas most of us might refer to the aggregate of television viewers as "the audience," employees of the industry habitually refer to them as "the market." The terminology is from commerce, not theater.

The buyers in the American marketplace are adults, especially the youthful and the middle-aged. It is we adults who purchase cars, select one brand of soap or another at our supermarkets, drink beer, smoke cigarettes, buy clothing. TV advertising, therefore, is beamed at adults, and the programs which occupy the time between commercials are intended to lure the adult viewer to the set. (Adolescents are also affluent spenders in the American marketplace, but it is well known that their preferred media are records, movies shown in theaters or drive-ins, and certain magazines. The adolescent spends less time watching television than do his parents or his younger siblings; he likes to spend his waking hours in the company of his peers, in settings away from his home. So TV advertising is only occasionally beamed to the teenager, and Madison Avenue has devised other approaches to persuade him to open his wallet.)

Children are not big spenders. They consume, but they do not purchase. Adults buy most of the clothing children wear, the breakfast foods they gulp down, the cars that transport them to music lessons and baseball games, the gasoline that runs those cars, the toys children find under the Christmas tree or aside the birthday cake. Children buy their own candy and soft drinks, but for most consumables they rely on adult suppliers.

So American television, the supreme sales medium, is not directed to children. The eight-year-old is not in the center of the thoughts of the TV writer or producer, and he never thinks of the three-year-old at all.

But children watch television. Two-year-olds toddle over to turn on the set, and by age three or four the American child is a regular TV watcher. The youngster graduating from high school today has spent many more hours in front of the tube than he has spent in the classroom. He started watching TV long before he reached the age of school attendance, he watched on weekends as well as on schooldays, and he learned from TV during summer vacations as well as during the academic year. We hear few complaints about truancy from TV, and the TV dropout is almost unknown.

As television viewers, young children are essentially intruders, outsiders, unexpected guests. They are voyeurs of a scene intended for other eyes, eavesdroppers on words meant for other ears.

True, a few TV programs are intended primarily for young children.

They include shows on what some members of the industry privately refer to as "the Saturday morning ghetto," and a few other shows in the late-afternoon hours on weekdays. Much of the best programming for children appears on noncommercial channels. On commercial television for children, sometimes labeled "kid-vid" in broadcasting circles, the advertising is frequent and unsubtle. It centers on children's products — toys, breakfast cereals — and reflects the ad man's hope that the youthful watchers will subsequently badger their parents to buy the advertised brands. Parental testimony indicates this hope is not vain.

Most of what young children watch on TV is programming intended for older viewers, for individuals who are more sophisticated in the ways of the world, more cognizant of the difference between fantasy and reality, more aware of the purposes of advertising. For these older viewers, what is learned on television is balanced against what has been learned from reading, in school, and from life experience. And the content of television is filtered through a more mature nervous system. For the very young viewer, on the other hand, the content of television is so different from anything in his life experience that he has no countervailing sources of information. An illiterate, he cannot turn to books or newspapers for other perspectives on the world. His own intelligence is still developing, and very likely it is unequal to the task of assessing and evaluating what he sees on TV.

For the very young child, television is *the* "early window" onto the world. Our authors have written a book about what the child views in that window, and how he is influenced by it. They draw on social psychological research about television's effects. They review survey research about who watches what. Included within their purview are the most recent studies as well as the "classics" from early TV research in the 1950s.

Like most social scientists, Drs. Liebert, Neale, and Davidson regard the television performance as instruction. They conceive of the child viewer as a pupil, learning from the content of television, and emulating the behavior he sees modeled by the people on TV. Although persons in the TV industry think they are purveying "entertainment" and "advertising" to the "market," social scientists believe it is more heuristic to say the TV industry is beaming education over the airwaves to learners.

The contrast is striking between the American public's preoccupation with governing the schooling of the nation's children and their indifference to governing what these same children learn from commercial television.

American public schools are led by elected local school boards. These mesh with county and state boards of education, whose members are public-spirited citizens, either elected or appointed by elected officials. At the federal level, we have a cabinet Secretary of Health, Education, and Welfare, and in his Department are the Office of Education, the National Institute of Education, etc.

The teachers and administrators of our public schools must meet carefully defined standards of professional competence before they are licensed to teach. Usually they are graduates of publicly supported institutions of higher education. These institutions are also governed by boards ultimately responsible to the electorate. Like the teachers, the curricular materials (textbooks, films, etc.) must pass careful review by committees before they may be revealed to the eyes of our impressionable youth.

Despite all his opportunities to influence his local schools, a parent may feel that they do not meet his children's needs. Such a parent has several options: move to another school district, enroll his child in a parochial school, enroll his child in a private secular school, or stay with the local schools and continue to work to change them.

If television is a form of education for children, as the authors and I believe, then we must ask how the governance of television compares with the governance of schools.

How may a citizen proceed to elect, reelect, or recall the persons who manage television? What power does the elected governor or state legislature have over what is taught by TV in their state? What are the federal regulatory agencies and how effective are they? Who is the relevant Cabinet officer? To what local or national officials may a parent complain when he is dissatisfied with what television is teaching his child?

What credentials of professional competence must a TV performer secure from a public licensing agency before he appears before the nation's young people as a mentor and model? What educational achievement does the public require of TV performers? Who are the public-spirited citizens who review the contents of the TV curriculum?

Finally, what are the options facing a parent who is dissatisfied with the TV offered in his community? Will moving to another district alter the programming available to his child? What are the TV equivalents of the parochial school or the private school?

Although the authors of *The Early Window* do not pose this issue in quite the stark terms I have chosen for dramatic emphasis, they do review the limited and oftentimes sorry history of efforts toward public government of TV broadcasting. The contrast between how effective the public is in influencing school instruction and how ineffective in influencing TV instruction will be vivid to the reader.

Drs. Liebert, Neale, and Davidson are unusually well qualified to evaluate research on children and television. Their own studies rank among the better ones in the research literature. The reader will find that they have been thoughtful in evaluating the evidence now available. Their scientific interest in the topic is joined by a compassionate concern for the well-being of children. Sometimes this leads them to speak forcefully. I honor them for their concern for children's welfare, and I am complimented that they asked me to introduce their book. I commend it to your thoughtful reading.

ALBERTA ENGVALL SIEGEL

Professor of Psychology,
Department of Psychiatry,
Stanford University, California,
January 1973

THE AUTHORS

Robert M. Liebert (Ph.D., Stanford University) is Associate Professor of Psychology, State University of New York at Stony Brook, N.Y. A principal investigator and overview writer for the National Institute of Mental Health's program on Television and Social Behavior, Dr. Liebert has published numerous articles on children's observational learning. He has coauthored four other books, including *Personality*, *Human Social Behavior* and *Developmental Psychology*.

John M. Neale (Ph.D., Vanderbilt University) is also Associate Professor of Psychology, State University of New York at Stony Brook, N.Y. He is a specialist in research methodology and abnormal behavior, and contributed a technical evaluation to the NIMH television reports. In addition to technical papers on these topics, Dr. Neale is coauthor of *Abnormal Psychology: An Experimental-Clinical Approach* and *Science and Behavior* (with Dr. Liebert).

Emily S. Davidson is a doctoral candidate in clinical psychology at State University of New York at Stony Brook, N.Y. Already having published several articles on both television and basic processes in imitative learning, Dr. Davidson is coauthor of two of the NIMH reports and a chapter—*Problems in behavioral research*—in Drs. Neale and Liebert's *Science and Behavior*.

This team, continuing its active interest in television, is currently studying further prosocial effects of television and the basic attentional processes underlying children's television usage.

PREFACE

It has been estimated that a child born today will, by the age of 18, have spent more time watching television than in any other single activity but sleep. What are, and will be, the effects of this continuous exposure?

The question is not a new one. It has been posed repeatedly since the advent of television sets as a common fixture in the home over two decades ago. Suggested answers, based both on simple opinion and on research which reflects varying degrees of sophistication and appreciation of the complexity of the issues, have ranged from confident statements that the medium's influence is uniformly undesirable to equally glib assertions that merely watching television entertainment fare can do little to shape children's attitudes and behavior.

Although literally hundreds of studies have been focused directly or indirectly on television and its effects on youngsters since the 1950s, the series of investigations recently completed for the Television and Social Behavior Program of the National Institute of Mental Health constitutes one of the most systematic and purposefully coordinated attempts to employ the efforts of a large group of researchers with relevant expertise and diverse viewpoints. Each of us played some role in that project, and thus had an opportunity to learn much about television's effects on children. Less expectedly, perhaps, we also learned much about politics, advertising, and the manner in which the news media gather and disseminate information. The research findings, it seemed, were clear and orderly but controversy, confusion, and misunderstanding appeared everywhere.

Anyone interested in going beyond newspaper accounts had to choose between terse, unsubstantiated summaries and 5000 pages of technical reports.

The purpose of this book, then, is to provide an account of the theory and research which now bears on television and children's attitudes, development, and behavior, and to explore the political and social questions which surround these issues. We have tried to write for those most likely to be concerned with television and its role in the future of our society: students, parents, men and women in public office. Where methodologically complex issues seemed to deserve mention, we have included them as optional discussion sections—designated "Answering Questions About Television"—and appearing in shaded print.

The business of social science and social policy is both complex and difficult on many counts; we have tried to explain rather than ignore these complexities, so as to provide a more complete understanding of our present state of knowledge and of the difficult road that must be followed by anyone who proposes changes in a large and successful industry.

In preparing this volume we received invaluable help from many sources. Drs. George A. Comstock and John P. Murray played vital roles in shaping much of the Surgeon General's project, and thus our own understanding of it (Dr. Comstock was also kind enough to permit us to use the title "The Early Window," which had been innovated by him at an American Psychological Association symposium in September 1971); secretarial services came from Patricia Ann Carl, Betty Hammer, and Adele Hollwedel, without whose efforts the manuscript would have been produced either very late or not at all; Elizabeth Kaplan and Elaine Brimer provided technical assistance, and their contributions are also acknowledged with thanks.

Our greatest debt, however, is to Dr. Rita W. Poulos, whose invaluable comments, constructive criticisms, and encouragement helped immeasurably in seeing the manuscript move from a rough draft to its present form.

ROBERT M. LIEBERT,
JOHN M. NEALE, and
EMILY S. DAVIDSON

State University of New York
Stony Brook, New York

1

FROM BIRTH TO MATURITY
IN TWENTY YEARS

On December 13, 1966, the National Broadcasting Company aired *The Doomsday Flight*. In the film, a bomb was placed aboard an airplane by a man who then telephoned the airline, offering to disclose its location in exchange for a huge ransom. Prior to the broadcast, the Air Lines Pilots Association had objected strenuously to the film, fearing that a television showing might lead to similar real-life actions. Its fears were justified. One bomb threat was received before the program was over; four additional threats were made in the next twenty-four hours and by the end of the week, eight more had been received by various major airlines. This represented an increase in threats of more than 800% over the previous month. When the movie was shown in Australia in May 1971, the results were equally dramatic. Victimized by a scheme which paralleled the televised events, Qantas Airlines paid $500,000 in ransom to safeguard the lives of 116 passengers en route to Hong Kong.

The *Doomsday Flight* incident is striking, but it is not a new or unique example of the power of television. Testimony before the U.S. Senate Subcommittee to Investigate Juvenile Delinquency in 1961 included the following documented instances[1]:

> *The Washington Daily News reported on December 10, 1958, that a juvenile court judge had told about a recent case where kids had committed a burglary by the professional method of forcing a skylight. The judge said that when he questioned the boys, they*

1

told him they had seen such a robbery committed on a television show.

The Evening Star, Washington, D.C., reported on December 18, 1958, that a 15-year-old youth had admitted in juvenile court that bizarre acts he committed against his neighbors had been inspired by television. Not only did he steal property, but he also sent ransom notes to his victims in exchange for the stolen material. He admitted stuffing papers in a woman's mailbox and the backdoor to her house and leaving a note, "See what happened, I'll do worse next time."

On July 9, 1959, the New York Journal-American reported that four young boys desiring a human skull for their club activities, broke into a Jersey City mausoleum, pried open a coffin and took one. They brought the skull to their clubroom where they desecrated it by sticking a lighted candle in it. Astonished police said the club members — seven boys, whose ages ranged 11 to 14 — got the idea from a television horror show.

The Chicago Tribune reported on November 22, 1959, that two Chicago boys had been arrested for attempting to extort $500 from a firm through a bomb threat. They threatened the owners and members of their families if police were notified. The boys . . . stated they got their idea from television.

According to the Reading Eagle, Reading, Pa., of March 2, 1960, a 16-year-old boy was arrested after neighbors spotted him entering the cellar of a home. He was wearing gloves and said he learned the trick of wearing gloves so that he did not leave fingerprints from television shows which he had watched.

A college athlete was arrested in Grand Junction, Colo., in April, 1960, after he had mailed letters threatening to kill the wife of a bank president unless he was paid $5,000. At the time of his arrest, he stated he got his idea from television shows . . . . Denver Post . . . April 10, 1960.

The New York Journal-American reported on December 22, 1960, that police arrested an 11-year-old who admitted having burglarized Long Island homes for more than $1,000 in cash and valuables. His accomplice was identified as a 7-year-old friend. The boy said he learned the technique of burglary by seeing how it was done on television. (pp.1923–1924)

Similar incidents are reported by Schramm and his associates from their investigations of the influence of television[2].

In a Boston suburb, a nine-year-old boy reluctantly showed his father a report card heavily decorated with red marks, then proposed one way of getting at the heart of the matter; they could give the teacher a box of poisoned chocolates for Christmas. "It's easy, Dad, they did it on television last week. A man wanted to kill his wife, so he gave her candy with poison in it and she didn't know who did it." (p. 161)

In Brooklyn, New York, a six-year-old son of a policeman asked his father for real bullets because his little sister "doesn't die for real when I shoot her like they do when Hopalong Cassidy kills 'em." (p. 161)

In Los Angeles, a housemaid caught a seven-year-old boy in the act of sprinkling ground glass into the family's lamb stew. There was no malice behind the act. It was purely experimental, having been inspired by curiosity to learn whether it would really work as well as it did on television. (p. 161)

A 13-year-old Oakville [California] boy, who said he received his inspiration from a television program, admitted to police . . . that he sent threatening notes to a . . . school teacher. His inspiration for the first letter came while he was helping the pastor of his church write some letters. When the minister left the office for an hour, the boy wrote his first poison pen letter. "I got the idea when I saw it happen on TV," he told Juvenile Sgt. George Rathouser. "I saw it on the 'Lineup' program." (p. 164)

These examples clearly tell us that at least certain kinds of programming may influence young children and adolescents dramatically. They raise a number of questions. How important is television in our children's lives? Who determines what is shown? Might we expect, despite the reports of deleterious effects, that television can have a beneficial influence? Do children merely copy what they see on television, or is there a more pervasive change in basic attitudes and belief systems? What kinds of people are most affected by television; how long do the effects last; what psychological mechanisms are involved?

In this book we will discuss each of these issues, what is already known about them, and the methods which are used to obtain such knowledge. For example, case studies like those cited above cannot be taken as conclusive proof of a relationship between television viewing and be-haviour[3]. Perhaps the youngsters would have behaved similarly even if they had not watched television. Thus, part of our discussion will focus on sounder methodologies for addressing the central question: What are the effects of television on young people? Finally, we will turn to the political implications of our explorations and consider the directions in which television might proceed. As a setting, we will first look at the medium itself: where it all started, where it is now, and who makes it the way it is.

THE ROOTS OF TELEVISION

Many of the basic technical advances necessary for audiovisual transmission were made long before television appeared on the public scene. The first television patent was issued in Germany — in 1884. As early as 1926, John L. Baird demonstrated a complete television system. In 1927 the American Telephone and Telegraph Company set up a dramatic long-distance telecast in the United States: as Herbert Hoover spoke in a studio in Washington, D.C., the sound and picture were received in New York — over 200 miles away.

Soon home television sets were being marketed. In 1939, the National Broadcasting Company began regularly scheduled telecasting, and within months other major U.S. networks were ready to start operation on a commercial basis; by 1941 some portion of the American public was enjoying the first broadcasts of college football, professional baseball, and boxing matches, and both national political conventions had been televised.

Then the expansion of commercial television slowed. The Federal Communications Commission decided to postpone further development until uniformity in the details of transmission could be established. Meanwhile, World War II broke out, usurping for itself both the technical and psychological energies of the country. But television was destined to grow. In 1947, after a debate about the feasibility of jumping into color broadcasting immediately (a proposal finally rejected by the FCC), a second period of massive expansion began. During the ensuing two-and-a-half decades, the medium mushroomed into the commercial giant that it is today.

A parallel rise was found in Britain; in 1936 the first public television program was broadcast from the London studio of the BBC. After several months of experimentation with two systems — the mechanical one which had been developed by Baird, and the electronic system of the Marconi

Corporation—the latter was chosen. Within a year 20,000 receivers were sold. Among the first performers were actress Greer Garson and playwright George Bernard Shaw. As in the United States, the growth of British television slowed markedly during the war. When it resumed in 1946 only 1300 receivers were still in operation, but five years later the number of sets reached the million mark.

TELEVISION AVAILABILITY AND USE

Availability in the United States

When television was introduced commercially on a large scale it was little more than a luxury for the wealthy. But it was a luxury with great appeal, especially for children. Those whose families had a television set quickly became popular; groups of neighborhood youngsters swarmed to the nearest TV-equipped home to soak up early cartoon and adventure offerings. Given this response, it is not surprising that within a decade virtually every American home had one television set and many had two or more. The swiftness of the rise in availability of television in the United States is shown in Fig. 1.1.

Availability in Other Countries

As seen in Table 1.1, the United States has no monopoly on its preoccupation with television. Twenty-five million television receivers can be found in the Soviet Union; Great Britain and West Germany each boast 17 million. Even impoverished and war-torn Egyptians own almost one million sets and the citizens of Buenos Aires recently petitioned to have their street lights dimmed rather than suffer a suspension in television programming to relieve an electric power shortage[5].

The Pervasive Influence of American Television

Of interest in considering television availability in other countries is the extent to which United States programming is exported. In Israel, 33% of the 43 non-news programs shown in one week originated in the United States[6]. Almost the same percentage (30%) of Great Britain's television is brought in from the United States[7]. Slightly less than half of Swedish television is imported, much of which is American produced[8]; New Zealand imports 75% of its programs, 60% of the imports (thus 45% of total programming) is American[9]. Japan and Formosa also import many

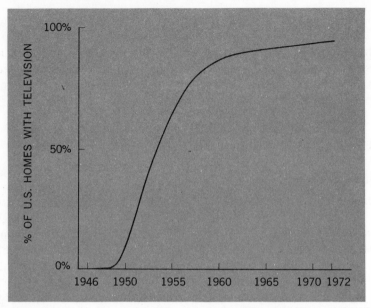

Fig. 1.1   Percentage of American homes with one or more television sets: 1946–1972 (Source: Based on data provided by Television Information Office[4]).

programs from the United States; of the 50 hours broadcasted each week by the latter, 18½ hours are devoted to American programming[10,11]. West Germany produces much of its own adult programming, but shows for children are mostly imports so the escapades of *Roadrunner* and similar American cartoon characters are familiar to German children and an issue of growing concern to their parents.

United States television has an impact on East European countries as well. According to one report: *"Dr. Kildare* is so popular in Poland that Communist Party meetings are no longer held on Wednesday nights." (p. 53) *Rawhide* is well received in Rumania, *Alfred Hitchcock* in Bulgaria[12].

To the extent that peoples around the world are exposed to United States productions, we might expect a relative shift — or at least a shaping — of their views of American life and culture. One government official, W. P. Dizard of the United States Information Agency, is well aware of this possibility[13]:

> *The amount of [commercial TV] exports, now approaching $100 million a year, is such that the television screen is becoming the main source of the "American image" for increasing millions*

Table 1.1 Growth of television, 1955–1964.

TV SETS

	Western Europe	Eastern Europe	Near East & South Asia	Africa	Far East	Latin America & Caribbean	Total
12/55	6,018,400	1,063,200	200	5,000	259,700	619,000	7,965,500
12/56	8,364,100	1,481,800	800	5,030	487,600	1,190,000	11,529,300
12/57	11,341,200	2,349,000	4,100	11,000	1,124,000	1,560,800	16,390,100
12/58	14,676,500	3,321,000	11,200	25,000	2,530,500	2,314,500	22,878,700
12/59	19,053,900	5,303,900	45,800	43,800	5,118,000	2,524,600	32,090,000
12/60	28,816,800	7,404,600	150,900	69,300	7,946,200	3,553,600	42,941,400
12/61	29,189,000	9,406,000	306,000	96,000	10,241,000	4,522,000	53,760,000
12/62	33,581,700	11,404,000	408,400	128,300	14,796,800	5,182,700	65,501,900
12/63	39,033,200	15,283,400	724,800	250,100	18,894,700	6,142,800	80,329,000
12/64	45,931,000	19,704,000	938,800	277,100	20,977,200	6,645,700	94,474,400

TV STATIONS

	Western Europe	Eastern Europe	Near East & South Asia	Africa	Far East	Latin America & Caribbean	Total
12/55	85	32	1	2	7	32	159
12/56	133	50	2	3	18	54	260
12/57	274	78	4	3	27	61	447
12/58	469	122	6	4	63	75	739
12/59	678	190	9	7	110	94	1,088
12/60	918	268	11	10	162	119	1,488
12/61	1,312	381	18	12	187	137	2,047
12/62	1,463	577	29	18	400	154	2,641
12/63	1,803	878	35	32	511	185	3,444
12/64	2,321	1,169	40	40	841	217	4,628

Source: United States Information Agency.

of people abroad .... Because our domestic television system is largely commercial, the quantity and quality of American television exports rests primarily in the hands of the private broadcasters. (p. 59)

What is the "American image" we are portraying? Robert Lewis Shayon has an idea[14].

My candidate for this season's most harmful television program is Mission: Impossible. *... The heroes of* Mission: Impossible, *for pay and at government instigation, interfere directly in the affairs of foreign nations with whom we are at peace and from whom no direct threat to our safety emanates. They break the laws of these nations.... In the United States the program series tends to legitimatize unilateral force for solving international problems at a time when our nation recognizes, or at least verbalizes, the desperate urgency of collaborative efforts among nations for world order. It pretends that individual Americans are morally impeccable when they break the laws of a foreign nation under the shield of our ideology ... in emergent nations the viewer may say: "The Americans are telling us, in these programs, that this is the way to run a society ...."* (p. 34)

Since Shayon wrote, the *Mission: Impossible* team has focused more of its efforts on domestic problems. But the lesson is the same: illegal and often brutal methods are appropriate means of dealing with crises.

Children's Use of Television

Broadcasting Yearbook 1971 estimates that the average American television set is turned on an average of 6 hours and 18 minutes per day[15]. Such a figure is not a true estimate of viewing time; few individuals actually watch that much and sets are often left on with no one present. Nonetheless, studies conducted almost since the beginning of commercial television are remarkably consistent in their overall estimates of viewing time. The general average seems to run between 2 and 3 hours per day for most children.

But blanket statements about "average" viewing time for the "average" child oversimplify somewhat our picture of the viewing habits of youth. Age plays a part in determining more specific viewing patterns, as do race, socioeconomic status, educational level, and intelligence.

Age

Despite a few reports that older children view more television than younger ones[16,17], and that there are no age differences at all[18,19], a different kind of relationship between age and viewing emerges from most studies. The British Broadcasting Corporation[20] reports more than 2 hours of viewing daily by children aged 5-11, with a drop to $1\frac{1}{2}$ hours in the early teens. Similar patterns are reported in America[21,22].

In a particularly intensive study, children in the primary grades were found to watch between 15 and 25 hours a week, older children about 25 hours, and high school students about 12 to 14 hours[23]. Other research showed that junior high school students watched over an hour more each day than those in senior high[24]. This general pattern—a slow increase of viewing into late childhood and a drop during adolescence—also appeared in the most recent major study, by Lyle and Hoffman[25], in which the viewing habits of children in a small town in Southern California were examined.

These investigators obtained interviews and one-day viewing records for 274 first-graders, and five-day television diaries from about 800 sixth-graders and 500 tenth-graders. The principal finding is clear: television is a major activity for children; most watched every day for at least 2 hours. Viewing peaked at the sixth grade and then dropped for the tenth-graders. These differences were due almost entirely to Sunday viewing: the first-graders watched about $2\frac{1}{2}$ hours, sixth-graders watched $6\frac{1}{2}$ hours and tenth-graders, $5\frac{1}{2}$ hours.

But there was also much individual variability in amount of viewing. Some sixth- and tenth-graders watched substantially more than the average—about 25% watched $8\frac{1}{2}$ hours on Sunday and $5\frac{1}{2}$ hours on school days. More than one-third of the first-graders watched 4 or more hours on a school day, while only 10% reported no viewing at all.

Not surprisingly, the younger children were more likely to watch during the earlier evening hours; first-grade viewing peaked at 8:00 p.m. although 10-15% were still watching at 9:30. About half the older children were watching at 9:00 and over 25% were watching at 10:30. The BBC study, cited above, also reported substantial numbers of children watching at 9:00.

Perhaps the pervasiveness of television can be seen even more clearly by moving from percentage figures to absolute numbers. Jennie McIntyre and James Teevan[26], citing the Violence Commission staff reports of 1969, have reminded us that "on one Monday during the period covered,

over five million children under the age of 12 . . . were still watching between 10:30 and 11:00 p.m. . . ."

Socioeconomic Status

With a few exceptions[18,27], results show a difference in viewing habits
between children in different social classes. Three teams working with
children of various ages have reported that children of lower socioeconomic status watched more than children of higher socioeconomic
status[28,29,30]. A similar pattern exists for both teenagers[29] and adults[31].

Ethnicity

Race and ethnic background appear to make no difference in the viewing of young children, but there are clear differences at older ages[25,32].
One team found that Mexican-American sixth- and tenth-graders, especially girls, watched more often than their Anglo peers[25]. In another study,
low income black teenagers were found to watch over 6 hours a day while
low income whites watched only $4\frac{1}{2}$ hours[29]. Similar results have appeared
for fourth- and fifth-grade children[33]. Although race is usually associated
with socioeconomic status (black children are more likely to be low in
social class), these differences appear regardless of economic background.

IQ

A few studies have related IQ scores to children's viewing habits.
Children with high IQ's view less television than those with lower
scores[18,34]. In one investigation, first-graders rated in the bottom third of
their classes by their teachers watched more television than children in
the middle and upper thirds; there were no differences for sixth-grade
children, but the slower tenth-graders also tended to watch more[25]. We
must remember, though, that children from higher social classes tend to
score higher on IQ tests, so the results do not necessarily mean that
television has an adverse influence on intellectual development.

Pre-TV: What Did People Do?

Since the average child spends more than 2 hours a day watching TV,
he necessarily spends about 2 hours less per day on other activities. When
television was introduced, radio listening and movie going were especially
hard hit[35,36]. The evidence concerning the consumption of printed
material — newspapers, books, and comics — is conflicting; some studies

reporting no change and others a decline[18,35,36,37]. Decreases in nonmedia related activities have also been examined. In the United States in 1951, when set ownership jumped from 20% to 50%, the amount of visiting and entertaining dropped from 25% on a typical day to only 13%[16]. Japanese youngsters not only spend less time with other media, they also go to bed later and spend less time on household chores and play[38].

The impact of television is not limited to children; it has been felt in every area of the day-to-day lives of adults too. It has been found that 60% of families have changed their sleeping patterns because of TV, 55% have altered meal times, and 78% use TV as an "electronic babysitter." Engineers in large metropolitan areas have even had to redesign city water systems because of the medium—to accommodate the drop in pressure caused by heavy lavatory use during prime time commercials[39].

Robinson[40] investigated the impact of television by comparing the daily activities of set owners and nonowners in 15 locations in 11 countries.* Noting that previous research had not adequately considered all the activities which might have been affected by television, he employed the technique of *time budgets*; he asked people to fill out diaries concerning all of their activities throughout a full 24 hour day.

He found consistency across all 15 sites for amount of time spent viewing (the range is from 70 minutes to 107 minutes per day) and percentage of owners who viewed on any one day (61–77%). Decreases in radio listening, book reading, and movie viewing were also found, but magazine and newspaper reading were relatively unaffected. Other activities which decreased were sleep, social gatherings away from home, other leisure activities (correspondence and knitting), conversation, and household care. In his report to the Surgeon General's Advisory Committee on Television and Social Behavior, Robinson observed:

> *Finally, it is of considerable interest to compare television with other innovations of the twentieth century. Comparing the amount of travel by owners of automobiles with that of nonowners, we were especially surprised that cross-nationally automobile owners on the average spent only six percent more time in transit than nonowners. While automobile owners were undoubtedly able to cover far more territory in the time they spent traveling, the overall shift is pale indeed compared with the 58 percent increase in media usage apparently occasioned by the influence of television.*

*Belgium, Bulgaria, Czechoslovakia, East Germany, France, Hungary, Peru, Poland, United States, West Germany, and Yugoslavia.

Cross-national data also indicate that time spent on housework is not grossly affected by the acquisition of home appliances like washing machines and dryers. Rather, it appears that time saved on these basic chores as a result of labor-saving devices is quickly channeled into other activities designed to improve the appearance of the home. Thus, at least in the temporal sense, television appears to have had a greater influence on the structure of daily life than any other innovation in this century. (p. 428)

Clearly then, television is a pervasive and important influence on society. But who makes the programs to which our young are exposed? What is the content of these offerings and what lessons do they teach? These are the questions to which we next turn our attention.

REFERENCES

1. U.S. Congress, Senate, *Effects on young people of violence and crime portrayals on television.* Part 10, Hearings before the Subcommittee to Investigate Juvenile Delinquency, Committee on the Judiciary, 87th Congress, 1961.
2. Schramm, W., Lyle, J., & Parker, E. *Television in the lives of our children.* Stanford, California: Stanford University Press, 1961. (With permission.)
3. Neale, J. M. & Liebert, R. M. *Science and behavior: An introduction to methods of research.* Englewood Cliffs, N. J.: Prentice-Hall, 1973.
4. *ABCs of radio and television.* New York: Television Information Office, 1972.
5. Mayer, M. *About television.* New York: Harper & Row, 1972.
6. Shinar, D. Structure and content of television broadcasting in Israel. In G. A. Comstock and E. A. Rubinstein (eds.). *Television and social behavior. Vol. I: Media content and control.* Washington, D.C.: U.S. Government Printing Office, 1972, pp. 493–532.
7. Halloran, J. D. & Croll, P. Television programs in Great Britain: Content and control (a pilot study). In G. A. Comstock and E. A. Rubinstein (eds.). *Television and social behavior. Vol. I: Media content and control.* Washington, D.C.: U.S. Government Printing Office, 1972, pp. 415–492.
8. Dahlgren, P. Television in the socialization process: Structures and programming of the Swedish Broadcasting Corporation. In G. A. Comstock and E. A. Rubinstein (eds.). *Television and social behavior. Vol. I: Media content and control.* Washington, D.C.: U.S. Government Printing Office, 1972, pp. 533–546.
9. Toogood, A. New Zealand broadcasting: A monopoly in action. *Journal of Broadcasting,* 1969, **14**, 13–24.
10. Gardner, L. W. A content analysis of Japanese and American television. *Journal of Broadcasting,* 1961, **6**, 45–52.
11. Tsai, M. K. Some effects of American television programs on children in Formosa. *Journal of Broadcasting,* 1969, **14**, 229–238.
12. The Red Tube, *Time,* January 12, 1968. (Reprinted by permission from *Time,* The Weekly Newsmagazine; copyright Time Inc.)
13. U.S. Congress, Senate, Hearings before the Subcommittee on International Organiza-

tions and Movements, "Modern Communications and Foreign Policy." 90th Congress, 1st Session, May 4, 1967, p. 59.

14. Shayon, R. L. Mission: Immoral. *Saturday Review*, November 19, 1966.
15. *Broadcasting Yearbook, 1971.* Washington. D.C.: Broadcasting Publications, Inc., 1971.
16. Cunningham & Walsh. *Videotown, 1948-1957.* New York: Cunningham & Walsh Publishers, 1958.
17. Battin, T. C. The use of the diary and survey method involving the questionnaire techniques to determine the impact of television on school children in regard to viewing habits and formal and informal education. University of Michigan, 1952, *Dissertation Abstracts*, 1952, **13**, 343.
18. Himmelweit, H., Oppenheim, A. N., & Vince, P. *Television and the child: An empirical study of the effects of television on the young.* London: Oxford University Press, 1958.
19. Maccoby, E. Television: Its impact on school children. *Public Opinion Quarterly*, 1951, **15**, 421-444.
20. British Broadcasting Corporation. *Facts and figures about viewing and listening, in twelve charts with a commentary.* London: British Broadcasting Corporation, 1961.
21. Mehling, R. Television's value to the American family member. *Journal of Broadcasting*, 1960, **4**, 303-313.
22. Riley, J., Cantwell, F., & Ruttiger, K. Some observations on the social effects of TV. *Public Opinion Quarterly*, 1949, **13**, 223-234.
23. Witty, P. Studies of the mass media, 1949-1965. *Science Education*, 1966, **50**, 119-126.
24. Chaffee, S. H., McLeod, J. M., & Atkin, C. K. Parent-adolescent similarities in television use. Paper presented at the meeting of the Association for Education in Journalism, Washington, D.C., 1970.
25. Lyle, J. & Hoffman, H. R. Children's use of television and other media. In E. A. Rubinstein, G. A. Comstock, & J. P. Murray (eds.). *Television and social behavior. Vol. IV: Television in day-to-day life: Patterns of use.* Washington, D.C.: U.S. Government Printing Office, 1972, pp. 129-256.
26. McIntyre, J. J. & Teevan, J. J., Jr. Television violence and deviant behavior. In G. A. Comstock and E. A. Rubinstein (eds.). *Television and social behavior. Vol. III: Television and adolescent aggressiveness.* Washington, D.C.: U.S. Government Printing Office, 1972, pp. 383-435.
27. Albert, R. & Meline, H. The influence of social status on the uses of television. *Public Opinion Quarterly*, 1958, **22**, 145-151.
28. Blood, R. Social class and family control of television viewing. *Merrill-Palmer Quarterly*, 1961, **7**, 205-222.
29. Greenberg, B. & Dominick, J. Racial and social class differences in teen-agers' use of television. *Journal of Broadcasting*, 1969, **13**, 1331-1334.
30. Friedman, M. Television program preference and televiewing habits of children as related to their socioeconomic status. Yeshiva University, 1957. *Dissertation Abstracts*, 1957, **22**, 1097.
31. Geiger, K. & Sokol, R. Social norms in television-watching. *American Journal of Sociology*, 1959, **65**, 174-181.
32. Murray, J. P. Television in inner-city homes: Viewing behavior of young boys. In E. A. Rubinstein, G. A. Comstock, & J. P. Murray (eds.). *Television and social behavior. Vol. IV: Television in day-to-day life: Patterns of use.* Washington, D.C.: U.S. Government Printing Office, 1972, pp. 345-394.

33. Greenberg, B. & Dominick, J. Television behavior among disadvantaged children. CUP Research Report, Department of Communication, Michigan State University, 1969.
34. Coffin, T. E. Television's impact on society. *American Psychologist*, 1955, **10**, 630–641.
35. Baxter, W. The mass media and young people. *Journal of Broadcasting*, 1961, **5**, 49–58.
36. Parker, E. B. The functions of television for children. Stanford University, 1960. *Dissertation Abstracts*, 1960, **21**, 2813–2814.
37. Parker, E. Television and the process of cultural change. *Journalism Quarterly*, 1955, **38**, 537–540.
38. Furu, T. *Television and children's life: A before-after study*. Tokyo: Japan Broadcasting Corporation Radio and Television Culture Research Institute, 1962.
39. Johnson, N. *How to talk back to your television set*. Boston: Little, Brown, & Co., 1967.
40. Robinson, J. P. Television's impact on everyday life: Some cross-national evidence. In E. A. Rubinstein, G. A. Comstock, and J. P. Murray (eds.). *Television and social behavior. Vol. IV: Television in day-to-day life: Patterns of use*. Washington, D.C.: U.S. Government Printing Office, 1972, pp. 410–431.

2

TELEVISION TODAY:
PRODUCTION AND CONTENT

Television production is a complex business, dependent on artistic, political, and economic factors. The process of producing a series is lengthy, expensive ($100,000 per half hour)[1], and risky (as the increasingly rapid turnover indicates).

Most series for adults begin with the testing of a pilot program; if the pilot is successful, the series goes into full-scale production. The producer handles the day-to-day work necessary to get a program on the air every week and, under the network's supervision, determines the content of the series. He selects the writers, and often provides the story line. Once the script is written, rarely does anyone except the producer change it. Directors are under too much time pressure to interfere with content decisions, and actors rarely exert their potential power[2].

Each network has a programming department which supervises the entire production process, with an eye toward securing the largest possible audience of 18 to 49-year-olds—the group which spends the most money and is, therefore, most likely to appeal to potential advertisers. Network censors work through the programming department, and try to protect the network from public outcry and government regulation[2].

The procedure for acquiring children's series is somewhat different from that used for adults'. Unlike adult shows, there are no pilots for children's programs. In adult fare, the producer sells 13 episodes for half a season, and then another 13 for the second half if the series is retained. These episodes may be rerun, but usually not more than once, during the summer. (A few highly successful series may be syndicated and shown again.) In contrast, when a network buys a children's series from a producer it signs a contract for 17 half hour shows; the network usually guarantees that each episode will be shown *6 times* over 2 years or, occasionally, *8 times* over 3 years. This incredible rerun practice, which would draw cries of outrage from adult viewers, is feasible because the audiences for children's shows change quickly. This year's audience is replaced by younger brothers and sisters next year. Although the profit margin on children's programming is smaller than that on adult series, once the series is sold it will almost never fail. Children's programs are also more likely to be syndicated; after being used by the network, they may then be shown for years[3]. So, as we shall see in Chapter 7, the overall profits which result from children's programming are staggering.

Ideas for series may come from the networks or from independent studios; rarely are they brought in from outside the industry. In any event, the network must approve of a show or it will never go on the air. So producers must consider the network from the outset, remembering that although children will watch the show, only adults can buy it. Producers rarely report any hesitation in complying with network directives; their aim is to please the buying customer—the network. Those who cannot accept the system are virtually forced to quit. Based on her extensive confidential interviews with producers, Muriel Cantor notes[3]:

> *Those producers who are committed to particular artistic and ethical values have trouble remaining in the commercial field. One well-known producer of a series presently on the air left the field of children's programming because he could not reconcile what he considered the networks' lack of social conscience with his own ideas of good craftsmanship and content.* (p. 266)

The networks get almost no feedback from the children who constitute their audience; they do not need it to serve their commercial interests. For a particular show, it makes little difference whether reaction is good or poor, since often all the programs in the series are made before even one is shown on the air. If a series is popular (i.e., has good Nielsen ratings) the characters will be used in merchandising and the music may be made into a record. Both practices make even more money for the producer. In addition, if one show is popular, the networks are more likely to buy a producer's next effort.

Although they do no research, producers do have some "ideas" about the nature of their audience. For example, they feel that children's attention span is limited, so that quick movement and loud noises are necessary. Most are unconcerned about the effects of their programs on the audience, arguing that it is the parent's responsibility — or the network's. Cantor found that some producers of action shows which were classified as children's programs by the National Academy of Television Arts even denied that children are part of their audience. One said[3]:

> We are not making a children's story. I don't think anyone in the business knows who their audience is. I think it is presumptuous of anyone to claim they know this. Kids don't know anything. They are not discerning. As long as we are on the air, I don't care. (p. 273, emphasis added)

In part because the networks like to "suggest" story lines, Saturday morning programming often has a theme. In the late 1960s the theme was war. Cartoons such as *Cool McCool* and *Colonel Bleep* showed super heroes defeating super bad guys, usually with complicated gadgetry. Sandwiched in were commercials, selling G. I. Joe army toys including a "ten-inch bazooka that really works" and gas masks "to add real dimension to your play battles." One observer remarked[4]:

> A visitor from another planet watching United States television for a week during the Vietnam escalation period might have concluded that viewers were being brainwashed by a cunning conspiracy determined to harness the nation — with special attention to its young — for war. Of course there was no conspiracy. Manufacturers were making things for which they saw a market, promoting them through advertising agents, producers, and broadcasters who believed in serving the client. (p. 268)

THE NETWORKS' INTEREST

The networks have a financial interest (subsidizing the production of many and owning some outright) in almost all the programs they show on their stations. Because of this, they largely determine program content, currently controlling about 93% of all prime time programming from start to finish. (In contrast, in the 1950s, considered by many to be the "Golden Age of Television," over half of the programs aired during prime time were independently produced.) Thomas Baldwin and Colby Lewis in their government sponsored research offer a succinct statement of what motivates network programming[2].

> The character of television programs is determined by the three networks' notions of what will appeal to large numbers of people,

sell products or services for advertisers, and not jeopardize the valuable licenses or the good will of affiliates by creating a negative audience response. (p. 294)

TELEVISION CONTENT: STEREOTYPES AND SOCIAL ROLES

In examining the content of television it is important to remember that entertainment fare necessarily does more than merely entertain us and our children; it communicates information about the social structure and it shapes attitudes about ourselves, others, and the world at large. George Gerbner, Dean of the University of Pennsylvania's Annenburg School of Communications, put it this way[5]:

Representation in the fictional world [of television] signifies social existence; absence means symbolic annihilation. Being buffeted by events and victimized by people denotes social impotence; ability to wrest events about, to act freely, boldly, and effectively, is a mark of dramatic importance and social power. Values and forces come into play through characterizations: good is a certain type of attractiveness, evil is a personality defect, and right is the might that wins . . . . The issue is rarely in doubt; the action is typically a game of personality, group identification, skill, and power . . . . Symbolic hurt to symbolic people and causes can show real people how they might use—or avoid—force to stay alive and advance their causes . . . . Several times a day, seven days a week, the dramatic pattern defines situations and cultivates premises about power, people, and issues. Just as casting the dramatic population has a meaning of its own, assigning "typical" roles and fates to "typical" groups of characters provides an inescapable calculus of chances and risks for different kinds of people. (p. 44)

In this section and the following one we will see that today's television entertainment offers many of these symbolic lessons to children—about occupations, racial groups, sex, and violence—much of it perpetuating a rather biased reflection of the world around us.

Sex Stereotypes

The most powerful group on television is the white, American male— fully half of all leading television characters fall into this category. He is usually young, middle-class, and unmarried. He is also likely to be involved in violence—especially as an aggressor rather than as a victim. And he is less likely than other characters to be punished for his aggression[5].

Women, of any ethnic or racial background, comprise only one-quarter of all television characters. They usually appear in a sexual context, in a romantic or family role; two of every three are married, were married, or are engaged. In contrast, most of the men are, and always have been, unmarried[5]. Further, while almost all male roles involve violence, only half of television's women participate in aggression. Women are less successful when they are involved in violence: they are more likely to be victims than aggressors; if they aggress, they are much *less* likely than men to get away with it. Other prejudices also appear; married women are less likely to be victims than single women and housewives are less often presented as villains than are women who are employed. Women are less law abiding than men; even heroines are portrayed as generally deviant from community values[6].

National and Ethnic Stereotypes

Misconceptions of national and ethnic groups are also fostered by television. In an early study, 80% of all characters were found to be white Americans; of the 20% remaining, Europeans (especially English and Italians) appeared most frequently[7]. India and Africa, with more than one-third of the world population, were almost entirely unrepresented, and China provided a mere 0.2% of the television population even though it represented 22% of the world's population. More recent research reveals that white Americans still comprise the overwhelming majority of television's fictional characters[5].

In an early study, minorities were more likely than Anglo-American whites to be law breakers; Italians were law breakers over half the time they were presented[7]. The same pattern has persisted. Gerbner's recent report to the government concluded that[5] . . .

> . . . *foreigners and those not identifiable as Americans, as a group, were [in 1969] increasingly more likely to become involved in violence and to pay a higher price for it than were the Americans.* (p. 58)

Television has been forced in the last ten years to reexamine its attitudes toward nonwhite groups, both in the United States and in other countries. One factor undoubtedly contributing to this change is the civil rights movement, with its demand for more black characters—and more prestige for them. Cedric Clark, a black psychologist at Stanford University, has examined the presentation of blacks on television[8]. He notes that statements about status and power have two components: recognition and respect. The first step toward full acceptance of a group is recognition of its existence—in terms of television, how often members of that group appear at all. The second step is respect—what kinds of roles the group gets. Are they dominant or submissive, educated or illiterate, good or bad, aggressor or victim?

In the 1950s, blacks were rarely presented at all and when they were, it was either as minor characters or as lovable but stereotyped buffoons (*Amos and Andy*). One West German professor, speaking of the early 1960s, remarked to us that he would never have known from American television that there were *any* black people in the United States.

In the last 5 years there has been some change in the number of blacks in leading roles. (*I Spy* was one of the first series to star a black man, Bill Cosby, in a nonstereotyped role.) But now blacks are largely presented as "regulators"[9]—staunch supporters of the *status quo* (e.g., in *Ironside* and *Mission Impossible*). This is a limited role, indeed, given the black experience in contemporary American society, but from Gerbner's analysis, it is not surprising. The purpose of TV drama, he says, is to teach lessons about the power structure or to change it in the service of the majority; we "need" blacks as law enforcers today. This portrayal presents the black community with the view that blacks do, and *should*, support the present social structure[9].

Occupational Roles

In the real world most people have jobs. Not so on television. Only 6 out of 10 television characters are clearly engaged in some occupational activity—and these are almost invariably upper and middle class. Less than one-tenth of the people on television are working class; when blue-collar characters do appear they are usually presented in a negative light[10,11]. Such presentations may contribute to the fact that blue-collar occupations continue to have a lower status in the eyes of our children than one would expect from income alone, and that people outside the United States—reinforced by our television entertainment—think of the United States as fostering values antagonistic to the working class. Those who are employed are most likely to be doctors, teachers, entertainers, or protectors of law and order — policemen, lawyers (trial, not corporate law), private detectives, and spies. Naturally the number of protectors is loosely paralleled by the number of enemies — criminals, counterspies, and saboteurs[5].

Smythe found that those in managerial-service occupations were greatly overrepresented[7]. Professionals, managers, officials, service workers, and servants comprised 51% of the television population (but only 11% of the actual United States population). In another study, DeFleur looked at occupational portrayals on prime time television (excluding westerns, quiz shows, cartoons, commercials, and news shows), using a criterion of at least 3 minutes of engaging in some recognizable job activity[6]. He found 436 characters with occupations, almost one-third (128) of which were related to law enforcement. Another 83 were in entertainment or in health and medical fields. DeFleur confirms other findings in that:

> *Among both males and females, professional workers were substantially overrepresented. Nearly a third of the labor force on television was engaged in professional occupations of relatively high social prestige. A similar concentration was noted in the category of managers, officials, and proprietors. This bias in the direction of the higher socio-economic strata is especially sharp for males . . . while nearly half the males in the actual labor force . . . held jobs in commerce and industry as operatives, craftsmen, and related workers, less than a tenth did so on television. . . . Thus, on the programs sampled there were more deep-sea divers than factory workers, more helicopter pilots than supermarket clerks, more night-club singers than salesgirls. (pp. 64–72)*

Those occupations which were presented were also likely to be stereotyped:

> *Lawyers were very clever, and usually legally unorthodox. Members of artistic professions were almost always temperamental and eccentric. Police officials were generally hardened, and often brutal. Private investigators were always resourceful and clearly more capable than the police. Nurses were cold and impersonal. Salesmen were glib. Journalists were callous. Taxi, bus, and truck drivers were burly and aggressive. (p. 71)*

Although the characters were stereotyped, the image was an atypical one: doctors, for example, were more likely to treat esoteric diseases or gunshot wounds rather than head colds and measles.

Smythe analyzed the various occupations according to how much they conform to American values[7]. Almost all the politicians (92%) who appeared in drama were law abiding; about 75% of the businessmen were. Teachers were the cleanest, kindest, and fairest; journalists the most honest. Scientists were least honest, least kind, and most unfair.

Preservation of Roles: Are the Stereotypes Justified?

Clearly, television does not mirror real world events, but it may reflect real world *values*. Head suggests that[10]:

> *Although the objectively measurable demographic norms of the fictional population differ widely from those of the real population, it does not necessarily follow that the more subjective norms of the two populations are equally dissimilar. Indeed, the very distortions of fact seem to represent an expression of values, wishes, and needs.*
>
> *Male dominance, for instance, may be no more extreme in the plays than it is in real society. Ours is said to be a youth culture, so that the emphasis on the most active age group in the plays is to be expected. The occupations which are least represented in the plays are the unglamorous, routine ones to which a large part of the real population is condemned.* (p. 189)

But the question remains: Whose values does the medium represent? The same author goes on to note:

> *Television, as a medium, appears to be highly responsive to the conventional, conservative values .... It does not appear that television, this most pervasive and intimate of the mass media, will often lend its support to the unorthodox. As conserver of the status quo, it will add tremendously to the cultural inertia. In an age of accelerated social change, this rigidity may prove disadvantageous. Communication has been described as "the cement which gives cohesion to social groups"; without mass communication, the intricate mechanism of modern societies could not function [Siebert, 1954]. This cement metaphor is perhaps unfortunate, since it suggests a hardening of the social structure into a monolith that is incapable of adapting to internal and external stresses. But if the trend toward static conformity is not countered through some of the influential channels of communication, this cement metaphor might prove all too apt.* (pp. 192–194)

VIOLENCE IN AMERICAN TELEVISION: YESTERDAY AND TODAY

Violence has always been a part of American television, but it has gradually and consistently increased in amount since the medium began[12]. The National Association of Educational Broadcasters reported to a Senate subcommittee on juvenile delinquency that there had been a 15% rise in violent incidents on TV entertainment from 1951 to 1953. Another study showed dramatic increases in 4 major cities in the percentage of prime time television devoted to violence-saturated action adventure programs—from an average of 17% in 1954 to about 60% in 1961. In one week of Los Angeles television in 1960 there were 144 murders, 13 kidnappings, 7 torture scenes, 11 planned (but unsuccessful) murders, 4 lynchings and a few more miscellaneous acts of violence, all occurring before 9:00 p.m.

By 1964, reported the National Association for Better Radio and Television, almost 200 hours per week were devoted to crime scenes, with over 500 killings committed[13]. The amount of time spent on crime drama showed a 20% increase over 1958 programming and a 90% increase since 1952. Over two-thirds of the violence shown in 1964 appeared before 9:00 p.m. In 1968, the same organization estimated that "the average child between ages 5 and 15 watches the violent destruction of more than 13,400 persons on TV"[14].

The list of studies reporting high amounts of violence could be lengthened. Indeed, the best documented fact about television is that it is violent.

Prime Time and Saturday Morning

One of the most accurate estimates of current levels of violence on television during prime time and Saturday morning is provided by Gerbner[5]. He first established the representativeness of programming for one week in October by comparing it to that of other times during the year. Then trained teams of observers watched each dramatic program shown during an October week selected in 1967, 1968, and 1969, recording the number of violent episodes. For the purposes of this study violence was defined as:

"The overt expression of physical force against others or self, or the compelling of action against one's will on pain of being hurt or killed." The expression of injurious or lethal force had to be credible and real in the symbolic terms of the drama. Humorous

and even farcical violence can be credible and real, even if it has a presumable comic effect. But idle threats, verbal abuse, or comic gestures with no real consequences were not to be considered violent. (p. 31)

Gerbner used two units of analysis: the play or skit, and the program hour. Although in most adult programs these units are equivalent, many children's programs present several plays per hour (e.g., as in a half hour cartoon program). Investigating more than the amount of violence, he also examined what types of programs contained the most violence, who acts violently, who is victimized by violence, and what happens to the participants.

The major results of this research are striking. In 1969 "about eight in ten plays still contained violence, and the frequency of violent episodes was still about five per play and nearly eight per hour" (p. 33). Further, the most violent programs were those designed exclusively for children — cartoons:

The average cartoon hour in 1967 contained more than three times as many violent episodes as the average adult dramatic hour. The trend toward shorter plays sandwiched between frequent commercials on fast-moving cartoon programs further increased the saturation. By 1969, with a violent episode at least every two minutes in all Saturday morning cartoon programming (including the least violent and including commercial time), and with adult drama becoming less saturated with violence, the average cartoon hour had nearly six times the violence rate of the average adult television drama hour, and nearly 12 times the violence rate of the average movie hour. (p. 36)

In fact, in 1967 and 1968 only two cartoons were nonviolent, and only one in 1969. The overall situation has not appreciably changed since 1954, when Smythe also found that children's programming contained three times as much violence as adult drama[7].

Gerbner has continued his analysis of network television dramas, and the data gathered in 1970 and 1971 are now available[15]. He summarizes the new findings: *"... new programs in 1971 spearheaded the trend toward more lethal violence by depicting record high proportions of screen killers."* (p. 3, *italics* added)

The level of violent programming over the 5 years studied can be seen in Fig. 2.1, which shows the percentage of programs containing violence. Figure 2.2 shows the number of violent incidents per program hour.

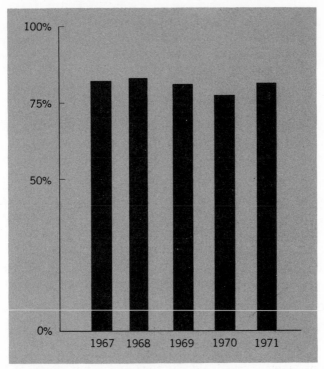

Fig. 2.1   The percentage of network dramatic programs containing violence: 1967–1971 (Source: Gerbner[15]).

Clearly, violence on television is not decreasing at any appreciable rate. Prime time drama is still (in the 1971–1972 season) overwhelmingly aggressive. The new figures are of special interest since they reflect a long history of unfulfilled network promises. Back in the mid-1960s network officials promised a sharp decrease in TV violence and then claimed the promise had been met; Gerbner's 1967 and 1968 data showed that it had not. The promise was reissued but, again, the appearance of Gerbner's 1969 data (published in 1972) showed little change. It was then claimed that substantial changes had certainly occurred during the 1970 and 1971 seasons. Now the data answer with unfortunate monotony: little change.

Other Violent Offerings

Network, prime time, and Saturday morning offerings do not constitute the entire picture — independent station and network daytime shows also contain a great deal of violence. Children usually watch an independent

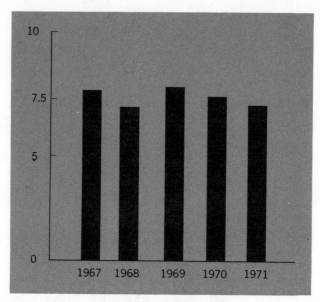

Fig. 2.2   The average number of violent episodes per program hour: 1967–1971 (Source: Gerbner[15]).

station when they come home from school; on it they are offered the sleaziest of violence-laced old cartoons and a pot-pourri of Westerns with almost as many ethnic slurs as commercials woven into them.

Likewise, although systematic analyses of daytime soap operas have not yet been undertaken, there is every reason to believe that they, too, are less than appetizing. One critic has written[16]:

> *During one six-month period when I watched . . . steadily, I found the incidence of crime very high and the suffusion of hatred almost unbearable; perhaps because the writers and actors lacked skill, the presentation of love or affection, rarely tried, was never convincing, and I felt something sinister as well as hateful coming off the screen.* (p. 107)

TELEVISION CONTENT IN OTHER COUNTRIES

Having considered television content in the United States, it is of interest to examine programming in other countries. Information is available on such diverse societies as Israel, Great Britain, and Sweden.

Israel

Israeli television is on the air only about four hours a day; these hours are "prime time" and, with the omission of the Saturday morning hours, can be considered equivalent to those studied by Gerbner in the United States[17]. When we compare television of the two countries, we find some striking differences. For instance, of 65 Israeli programs, only 9 were of the fiction drama type which constitutes much of American television, and which contains much of its violence. Eight fell into the entertainment category, while 26 were classified as news, and 22 as informational. More directly relevant, the average number of violent episodes for all Israeli programs was 0.8, compared to 5.0 for the United States (the definition of violence was quite similar to Gerbner's). Children's programming was *less* violent (0.4) than adults' (1.1).

The contrast is particularly intriguing considering that many programs shown in Israel are purchased from the United States. Decision-makers in Israeli television deliberately influence the amount of violence shown, considering it acceptable only when it is dramatically necessary or expresses artistic truth. They are free to do this, in part, because Israeli television has no commercials. When violence does appear, it apparently resides in programming purchased from the United States. Israel produced 21 programs, two of which contained at least one violent episode, and the United States supplied 14, 12 of which contained violence[17].

Great Britain

An early look at British programming, prior to the introduction of commercial television, revealed that it was less than half as violent as American fare but that, as in the United States, children's programs were more violent than adults' programs[18]. Plays about crime were usually aimed at adults[19].

We can examine the findings of Halloran and Croll to see whether this trend has continued[20]. Their study consisted of an analysis of the programs shown between 4 and 11 p.m. during one week in April 1971, on two BBC channels and one commercial network. Of the 176 programs broadcast, 79 were drama, 56 news information, and 41 sports and variety. Sixty-seven percent of the drama programs were produced in Britain; the remainder came primarily from the United States.

About half of the dramas contained violence (according to Gerbner's definition), occupying almost two-thirds of the program hours. There were approximately 4 violent incidents per hour (in contrast to American television with 7 per hour in 1971)[15]. The most violent programs were cartoons, with a remarkable 34 incidents per hour; of the 6 cartoons shown, 5 were of American origin. Crime, action, and adventure programs were next, with an average of about 7 per program and 8 per hour; it can be noted that American imports are twice as likely to be of this type (38%) as are British programs (19%).

British television wins high praise from critics, especially Americans. Brian Wenham, writing for the *New Republic* remarks that "television output . . . on its good nights is said to be unrivaled in the world . . . ." (p. 20)[21] M. J. Arlen (*The New Yorker*) comments[22]:

> [*British television*] *can be sharp and bright and funny. Mostly, it seems fairly intelligent, and, I should imagine, useful to the nation . . . and easy to live with which . . . is no small potatoes.* (pp. 187–188)

A number of factors contribute to such excellence. Many of the outstanding actors in Britain, including members of the National Theatre Company and the Royal Shakespeare Company, perform for minimum wages, making top-level talent easily available. A second factor is the lack of commercial or government control of the BBC, and limited control of content by sponsors even on the commercial stations. The end result is programs such as *The Forsyte Saga*, which has been well received in the United States.

Sweden

Sweden's only network was established by law, and television is broadcast over two channels: "TV 1" is on the air about 40 hours per week, "TV 2" about 28. Dahlgren analyzed the average percentages of various types of programs from November 1969 to June 1970. Although the two channels differed somewhat in their programming, the overall amount of fiction is quite small relative to the United States. Entertainment variety shows, quiz programs, and amusement "documentaries" that are very popular in the United States, consumed only 2% of total air time on TV 1 and less than 4% on TV 2. Children's programs constitute 13% and 11% of air time for the two channels respectively[23].

What about violence? Dahlgren[23] performed a content analysis of programming during one week in May 1971 and ". . . soon discovered that there was so little violence . . . that an elaborate schedule became meaningless." (p. 544) The nine programs which contained any violence at all occupied only about 14% of total air time, and the "violence" often appeared to be mild by American standards – a plane crash due to negligence, or wild moving about (not directed against anyone in particular) to display severe schizophrenia. A few foreign-made programs contained more standard violence, and two nonfiction shows aired during the week displayed considerable violence. One contained footage of street riots; the second, a discussion panel following the showing of an American war movie, used film clips from three other war movies.

In Sum

In a summary analysis, Gurevitch compared the data from the studies of Swedish, American, Israeli, and British television[24]. The amount of violence varied according to the type of program. Cartoons were most violent in both American and British schedules; all the British cartoons and 98% of American cartoons contained violence. Films were also high in violence in the United States, Britain, and Israel. What appears to be the critical feature in determining the amount of violence is the type of program, regardless of country of origin (although American television appears to have a slight edge). United States television leads in amount of violence simply because it shows a much larger proportion of programs which feature violence, such as crime-adventure shows and cartoons.

VIOLENCE ON TELEVISION: REALITY AND PERCEPTIONS

In justifying the frequent portrayal of violence on American television, two statements are often heard: that there is as much violence in the "real world" as on television and that children do not perceive television entertainment as a reflection of the real world anyhow. Regarding the former, one producer said[2]: "There's not one-hundredth as much violence on TV as there is in the society." (p. 299) His assertion is patently false.

A Closer Look at Violent Content

Probably the most important stereotype as far as violence is concerned is the "cops and robbers." In 1967 and 1968 *all* TV criminals were involved in violence – either by being aggressive, being attacked, or both[5]. Television has so inured us to violence that, at first glance, it may appear reasonable that most criminals should be portrayed as violent. But most real world crimes involve money and property – the criminal may never even see, much less physically injure, the property owner.

The role of law enforcement officers in all drama is relatively small (about 20% of general dramatic episodes), but that role is exceedingly, and increasingly, violent. Law officers were violent in about 60% of their appearances in 1967, 72% in 1968, and 77% in 1969. Law men became more likely to inflict violence, without being aggressed against themselves. In real life the great majority of law enforcement officers rarely, if ever, fire their guns, except on the target range.

Criminal activity and efforts to stop it do *not* make up the bulk of violence on television. Rather, it is noncriminals, otherwise admirable citizens, who use violence to solve their problems. As Gerbner puts it[5]:

> *Illegals naturally inflicted proportionately more violence. But about nine-tenths of all violence and at least three-quarters of all killing did not involve criminals . . . . due process of law was indicated as a consequence of major acts of violence in only two of every ten violent plays.* (p. 56)

It appears, then, that the law — justice and arbitration in the courtroom — almost never succeeds in the world of television. Violence, on the other hand, almost inevitably works — at least for its white male perpetrator.

How well does television violence reflect that of the "real" world? Clark and Blankenburg compared violence, as estimated from *TV Guide* synopses, to the Uniform Crime Reports of the F.B.I.[25] They found almost no relationship. Comparing the relative frequency of types of crimes, a different investigator reported[10]:

> *The crimes emphasized in the dramas are relatively infrequent in real life. Homicide [for example] constitutes 14 percent of the crimes in the television society; but, in 1951, only 0.65 percent of the crimes reported to the police were classified as homicide.* (p. 188)

Perception of Reality

Although television entertainment does not provide an accurate picture of the real world, many children and adolescents believe that it does. Lyle and Hoffman questioned first-, sixth-, and tenth-grade students[26]. About half the first-graders felt that the people on TV were like the people they knew. The older children were more skeptical, but large percentages believed that TV characters and real people were alike most of the time. Lyle and Hoffman also found that Mexican-American or black children were less skeptical than Caucasian youngsters. Disadvantaged children are also likely to perceive television, or at least television violence, as lifelike[27].

One group of investigators questioned fourth- and fifth-grade children about the relationship between television and reality[28]. By their own reports, children were uncertain as to the reality of what they were viewing. Other scientists report that many children associate TV violence with real-life violence—and that these children were more likely to be aggressive themselves[29]. A second report states that 46% of the adolescents felt crime shows were likely to "tell about life the way it really is."[30] McIntyre and Teevan also found that many boys perceive television violence as realistic, and that these boys tend to be more deviant[31]. About two-thirds of their respondents thought that both situations and characters on their favorite programs were true to life; highly violent programs were considered as realistic as low to moderately violent shows.

We have seen that violence is the most prevalent theme of television entertainment, at least for offerings produced in the United States. What effects, if any, do these endless presentations of murder and mayhem have on children? The following chapters address that question.

REFERENCES

1. Gerbner, G. The structure and process of television program content regulation in the United States. In G. A. Comstock and E. A. Rubinstein (eds.). *Television and social behavior. Vol. I: Media content and control.* Washington, D.C.: U.S. Government Printing Office, 1972, pp. 386–414.
2. Baldwin, T. F. & Lewis, C. Violence in television: The industry looks at itself. In G. A. Comstock and E. A. Rubinstein (eds.). *Television and social behavior. Vol. I: Media content and control.* Washington, D.C.: U.S. Government Printing Office, 1972, pp. 290–373.
3. Cantor, M. G. The role of the producer in choosing children's television content. In G. A. Comstock and E. A. Rubinstein (eds.). *Television and social behavior. Vol. I: Media content and control.* Washington, D.C.: U.S. Government Printing Office, 1972, pp. 259–289.
4. Barnouw, E. *A history of broadcasting in the United States, Vol. III—from 1953: The image empire.* New York: Oxford University Press, 1972. (Copyright© 1972 by Erik Barnouw.)
5. Gerbner, G. Violence in television drama: Trends and symbolic functions. In G. A. Comstock and E. A. Rubinstein (eds.). *Television and social behavior. Vol. I: Media content and control.* Washington, D.C.: U.S. Government Printing Office, 1972, pp. 28–187.
6. DeFleur, M. Occupational roles as portrayed on television. *Public Opinion Quarterly,* 1964, **28**, 57–74. (Reprinted with permission.)
7. Smythe, D. W. Reality as presented by television. *Public Opinion Quarterly,* 1954, **18**, 143–156.

8. Clark, C. C. Race, identification, and television violence. In G. A. Comstock, E. A. Rubinstein, and J. P. Murray (eds.). *Television and social behavior. Vol. V: Television's effects: Further explorations.* Washington, D.C.: U.S. Government Printing Office, 1972, pp. 120–184.

9. Clark, C. C. Communication, conflict, and the portrayal of ethnic minorities: A minority perspective. Unpublished manuscript, Stanford University, 1972.

10. Head, S. Content analysis of television drama programs. *Film Quarterly*, 1954, **9**, 175–194. © 1954 by The Regents of the University of California. Reprinted from *Film Quarterly* by permission of The Regents.)

11. Gentile, F. & Miller, S. M. Television and social class. *Sociology and Social Research*, 1961, **45**, 259–264.

12. Greenberg, B. S. The content and context of violence in the mass media. In R. K. Baker and S. J. Ball (eds.). *Violence and the media.* Washington, D.C.: U.S. Government Printing Office, 1969, pp. 423–452.

13. National Association for Better Radio and Television. *Crime on television: A survey report.* Los Angeles: National Association for Better Radio and Television, 1964.

14. National Association for Better Radio and Television. Cited in L. Sabin, Why I threw out my TV set. *Today's Health,* February 1972. (Published by The American Medical Association.)

15. Gerbner, G. The violence profile: Some indicators of the trends in and the symbolic structure of network television drama 1967–1971. Unpublished manuscript, The Annenberg School of Communications, University of Pennsylvania, 1972.

16. Seldes, G. A. *The public arts.* New York: Simon and Schuster, 1956.

17. Shinar, D. Structure and content of television broadcasting in Israel. In G. A. Comstock and E. A. Rubinstein (eds.). *Television and social behavior. Vol. I: Media content and control.* Washington, D.C.: U.S. Government Printing Office, 1972, pp. 493–532.

18. Suchy, J. British television and its viewers. *Journalism Quarterly*, 1954, **31**, 466–472.

19. Himmelweit, H., Oppenheim, A. N., & Vince, P. *Television and the child: An empirical study of the effects of television on the young.* London: Oxford University Press, 1958.

20. Halloran, J. D. & Croll, P. Television programs in Great Britain: Content and control (a pilot study). In G. A. Comstock and E. A. Rubinstein (eds.). *Television and social behavior. Vol. I: Media content and control.* Washington, D.C.: U.S. Government Printing Office, 1972, pp. 415–492.

21. Wenham, B. Public TV and the networks, *The New Republic*, May 13, 1967. (Reprinted by permission of THE NEW REPUBLIC © 1967, Harrison-Blaine of New Jersey, Inc.)

22. Arlen, M. J. The Air: The telly. *The New Yorker*, May 13, 1967.

23. Dahlgren, P. Television in the socialization process: Structures and programming of the Swedish Broadcasting Corporation. In G. A. Comstock and E. A. Rubinstein (eds.). *Television and social behavior. Vol. I: Media content and control.* Washington, D.C.: U.S. Government Printing Office, 1972, pp. 533–546.

24. Gurevitch, M. The structure and content of television broadcasting in four countries. In G. A. Comstock and E. A. Rubinstein (eds.). *Television and social behavior. Vol. I: Media content and control.* Washington, D.C.: U.S. Government Printing Office, 1972, pp. 374–385.

25. Clark, D. G. & Blankenburg, W. B. Trends in violent content in selected mass media. In G. A. Comstock and E. A. Rubinstein (eds.). *Television and social behavior. Vol. I: Media content and control.* Washington, D.C.: U.S. Government Printing Office, 1972, pp. 188–243.

26. Lyle, J. & Hoffmann, H. R. Children's use of television and other media. In E. A. Rubinstein, G. A. Comstock, and J. P. Murray (eds.). *Television and social behavior. Vol. IV: Television in day-to-day life: Patterns of use.* Washington, D.C.: U.S. Government Printing Office, 1972, pp. 129–256.

27. Greenberg, B. S. & Gordon, T. F. Children's perceptions of television violence: A replication. In G. A. Comstock, E. A. Rubinstein, and J. P. Murray (eds.). *Television and social behavior. Vol. V: Television's effects: Further explorations.* Washington, D.C.: U.S. Government Printing Office, 1972, pp. 211–230.

28. Greenberg, B. S., Ericson, P. M., & Vlahos, M. Children's television behaviors as perceived by mother and child. In E. A. Rubinstein, G. A. Comstock, and J. P. Murray (eds.). *Television and social behavior. Vol. IV: Television in day-to-day life: Patterns of use.* Washington, D.C.: U.S. Government Printing Office, 1972, pp. 395–409.

29. McLeod, J. M., Atkin, C. K., & Chaffee, S. H. Adolescents, parents, and television use: Adolescent self-report measures from Maryland and Wisconsin samples. In G. A. Comstock and E. A. Rubinstein (eds.). *Television and social behavior. Vol. III: Television and adolescent aggressiveness.* Washington, D.C.: U.S. Government Printing Office, 1972, pp. 173–238.

30. McLeod, J. M., Atkin, C. K., & Chaffee, S. H. Adolescents, parents, and television use: Self-report and other report measures from the Wisconsin sample. In G. A. Comstock and E. A. Rubinstein (eds.). *Television and social behavior. Vol. III: Television and adolescent aggressiveness.* Washington, D.C.: U.S. Government Printing Office, 1972, pp. 239–313.

31. McIntyre, J. J. & Teevan, J. J., Jr. Television violence and deviant behavior. In G. A. Comstock and E. A. Rubinstein (eds.). *Television and social behavior. Vol. III: Television and adolescent aggressiveness.* Washington, D.C.: U.S. Government Printing Office, 1972, pp. 383–435.

3

TELEVISION AND AGGRESSION: THE PROBLEM AND THE ISSUES

When parents are asked what programs they would like to prevent their children from watching, almost two-thirds answer that they would like to eliminate those containing crime, violence, and horror[1]. One reason, suggested by Eve Merriam, is that such shows teach children that violence is just another form of entertainment[2]. As she puts it:

> ... they are becoming passively jaded. As a kind of self-protection, they develop thick skins to avoid being upset by the gougings, smashings and stompings they see on TV. As the voice of reason is shown to be a swift uppercut to the chin, child viewers cannot afford to get involved, for if they did, their emotions would be shredded. So they keep "cool," distantly unaffected. Boredom sets in, and the whole cycle starts over again. Bring on another show with even more bone-crushing and teeth-smashing so the viewers will react. (p. 45)

Similarly, psychiatrist Fredric Wertham is concerned that while TV violence blunts emotional responses to both entertainment and real-life aggression, it also serves as a uniquely effective "school for violence."[3]

> Whether crime and violence programs arouse a lust for violence, reinforce it when it is present, show a way to carry it out, teach the best method to get away with it or merely blunt the child's (and adult's) awareness of its wrongness, television has become a school for violence.

34

In this school young people are never, literally never, taught that violence is in itself reprehensible. The lesson they do get is that violence is the great adventure and a sure solution, and he who is best at it wins. (p. xii)

THE LESSON OF TELEVISION: VIOLENCE WORKS

As we saw in Chapter 2, violence is a major part of television offerings. However, a mere counting of such incidents does not shed light on what lessons these portrayals of violence may teach. One way we can obtain this information is to examine the manner in which characters on television achieve their goals.

In one investigation, 18 programs were studied, 6 in each of three categories—adult programs, "kidult" programs (programs where the child or teenage audience comprised at least 30% of the total audience), and children's programs which consisted largely of cartoons[4]. In all 3 program types, violent methods were the ones most frequently used in goal attainment. And violence and other illegal activities worked. When goal achievement methods were further analyzed for degree of success, it became clear that the most successful methods were *not* those in the socially approved category. Simply, then, television programming—both aimed at children and at adults—is presenting an antisocial system of values.

Himmelweit, Oppenheim, and Vince found that British television consistently teaches that self-confidence and toughness are necessary to achieve success—that goodness of character is not enough. Even good people on TV often resort to violence as an inevitable part of life[5]. Among the explicit values expressed are that both law enforcers and criminals will bully and cheat if necessary, and that appearances are deceptive. The authors note, in contrast, the absence of positive lessons on television:

A whole range of values, however, never finds expression in Westerns—those to do with family, work, education, and manners. The characters do not need them in their way of life; they are rarely encumbered by parents, wives, or children, and seldom eat or go into their homes . . . . (p. 184)

Recently Gerbner summarized the values now presented on American television[6]:

To be able to hit hard and to strike terror in the hearts of one's opponents—that makes one count when the chips are down. The

*battered hero triumphs over evil by subduing the bad guy in the
end. The last man to hit the dust confirms his own flaw of character
and cause. Hurting is a test of virtue and killing is the ultimate
measure of man. Loss of life, limb, or mind, any diminution of the
freedom of action, are the wages of weakness or sin in the symbolic
shorthand of ritual drama.* (p. 44)

Can Violence Viewing Blunt Children's Sensitivity?

The values presented on television may actually change children's
perceptions. One study conducted by Martin Rabinovitch and his associates showed that sensitivity to violence may be affected directly by
television[7]. Sixth-grade children saw either a violent program (an episode
of *Peter Gunn*) or a nonviolent one (an episode from *Green Acres*). Then
each child was tested using a stereoscopic projector, in which different
images can be presented simultaneously to each eye so quickly that only
one is seen. The two images were very similar but one was violent and one
nonviolent (*see* Table 3.1). For example, one slide showed one man hitting
another over the head with a gun; the corresponding nonviolent slide

Table 3.1 Description of pairs of slides used in free response measure of violence perception.

Number	Violent slide	Nonviolent slide
1	One man hits the other over the head with a gun.	One man helps the other pound a pole in the ground with a gun butt.
2	One man shoots the other with a rifle.	Both men walk. One carries a rifle.
3	One man pushes the other off a bridge.	Both men walk on the bridge.
4	One man kicks the other off a merry-go-round.	Both men ride on a merry-go-round.
5	One man hits the other over the head with a book.	One man shows the other something in a book.
6	One man, tied up, tries to hit the other man.	One man holds a rope. The other looks at the rope.
7	One man hits the other over the head with a car jack.	One man helps the other take a car jack out of the car trunk.
8	One man hits the other over the head with a rock.	Both men help to lift a rock.
9	One man holds the other and takes money at gunpoint.	One man gives the other man money from his wallet.

Source: Rabinovitch, McLean, Jr., Markham, and Talbott (1972).

Fig. 3.1   Sample slide pair from Rabinovitch's study of the perception of violence (Source: Courtesy of Dr. Martin Rabinovitch).

showed a man helping another pound a pole into the ground with a gun butt. Another pair contrasted hitting someone with a book and showing the book to him (*see* Fig. 3.1). After each slide pair was presented, the child wrote down a description of what he had seen. Those who had seen the episode from *Peter Gunn* were less likely to report violence, suggesting that they had become at least temporarily less sensitive to it.

Reducing children's sensitivity to violence is just one of the effects that violent TV fare can have on young people. To examine its other effects, we must turn to a more detailed examination of psychological theory and research.

ANSWERING QUESTIONS ABOUT TELEVISION: THE EXPERIMENTAL METHOD*

The experimental method involves the manipulation of some experience (called the *independent* variable) and then the measurement of some aspect of behavior (the *dependent* variable). The major purpose is to determine if the changes in the independent variable produce changes in the dependent variable; that is, to determine whether there is a causal relationship between the two. An additional goal is to insure that *only* the independent variable could have caused the differences—to eliminate alternative interpretations of the results. For example, an investigator may be interested in the effects of praise on children's friendliness. Suppose he asks a teacher to enthusiastically praise children in her class for a week, and finds that on the last day all are friendly. Can he now say that praise increases friendliness? No. Several so-called rival hypotheses can explain his data; for example, the weather may have been nicer on the day of testing, the class lessons may have been easier, or the weekend may have been nearer. Any of these factors might have put everyone in a good mood, thereby making them friendlier. The experimenter must try to eliminate these rival hypotheses, and usually does so by employing a *control group*.

The simplest kind of experiment, then, involves two groups: one, the experimental group, receives the experience (or "treatment") of interest while the other, the control group, does not. When the experiment is concluded, the investigator will have one or more scores for each

---

*This section and others like it throughout this book are designed to explain the more technical details of social scientific research on which our present understanding rests. They are all set off in gray shading, and may be passed over by readers who are less interested in the methods which have been used to reach our conclusions.

participant—measures of the dependent variable. He will then compare the average scores of the two groups. If the children who received praise are friendlier than those who did not, nice weather presumably had nothing to do with it, since everyone benefited from the sunshine.

But the researcher wants to go yet a step further and ask: can I *infer* from the experiment that other children who did not actually participate in this research will also be similarly affected by praise? Or could my results have appeared, with the particular children who did participate, simply by chance? It is this pair of questions, regarding inference to the larger *population* of children who were not studied directly, that is critical.

Obtaining the answer involves performing an appropriate statistical test* that tells us the probability that the difference between the experimental and control groups is due only to chance. If—and only if—the probability is low do we infer that the results hold in the larger population of untested individuals. In behavioral research, the probability level is acceptably low when the likelihood is 5 or less in 100 that the obtained results would have occurred by chance. This level is called the 0.05 level of significance and is commonly written, "$p < 0.05$" and read "probability less than five percent." All of the findings put forth as "significant" in this book have met this stringent criterion.

OBSERVATIONAL LEARNING

Research concerning television's effects on children focuses on a portion of a larger area of scientific investigation, *observational learning* or the way in which the behavior of children (and adults) changes as a result of exposure to the actions and values of others. Studies of observational learning demonstrate that such exposure can change varied behaviors, such as a child's willingness to aid others[8], his ability to display self-control[9], and his learning of language rules[10]. Observation of others on film can increase learning of unfamiliar behaviors[11], increase sharing[12], and decrease fear[13, 14]. Because observational learning is implicated in so many aspects of the socialization process, professionals and laymen alike are interested in television as an observational teacher. We must examine the concept more closely.

Observational learning is a complex phenomenon involving a number

---

*A description of such tests and a further explanation of the logic which underlies them may be found in Neale and Liebert's *Science and behavior: An introduction to methods of research*. (Prentice-Hall, 1973).

of processes. The terminology can get confusing, so first a few definitions are in order.

Modeling

Modeling refers to the observed behavior of others whether demonstrated directly or through films, television, or print. The first type is known as *live* modeling; the second, which includes the behavior of others as presented by television, is known as *symbolic* modeling.

Learning versus Acting on What Has Been Learned

The oldest and most basic distinction in the study of observational learning was introduced by Albert Bandura and Richard Walters in 1963[15]. They differentiated the ability to recall or reproduce previously unfamiliar responses from the spontaneous performance of an observed act. A child may learn or *acquire* a particular behavior sequence, such as a new way to torment his little brother, without necessarily putting it into practice or *accepting* it as a guide for his own actions. Obviously, however, acquisition is a prerequisite to acceptance. So one possibility suggested by the distinction is that a child may learn a novel set of responses, which he will not immediately perform. But when he is placed in a different situation later, for example, when he is angry or frustrated, he may bring these new behaviors into play.

Imitation and Disinhibition

Observational learning can have two types of effects: direct imitative/counter-imitative and inhibitory/disinhibitory. In direct imitation, the child attempts to copy the model's behavior as closely as possible. In direct counter-imitation, he actively avoids copying; for example, staying away from a hot stove after seeing a playmate burned by touching it.

Disinhibition, sometimes called response facilitation, refers to performance of behaviors which fall into the same *class* as the modeled behavior, but are different in particulars. For example, a child who has observed his parents giving clothes to the Red Cross may then share his toys with his sister; he has emulated the idea of sharing. Disinhibition is of particular importance regarding observational learning of violence. Much of the violence found on television involves the use of weapons, especially guns; since they are generally unavailable to children, direct imitation is impossible. But disinhibition of aggression might still occur, producing an increase in other types of aggressive behavior.

Alternatively, one might argue that watching violence on TV will actually inhibit the performance of aggression by youngsters if, for example, it either drains off aggressive impulses, shows the horror of violence, or convinces the observer that he will be punished for aggressive behavior.

Observational Learning as a Three Step Process

From the discussion so far, it can be seen that observational learning involves three steps; (1) the observer's exposure to modeling cues, (2) his acquisition and recall of what he has seen, and (3) his acceptance of the model's behavior as a guide for his own. These three steps and the alternatives possible at each step are presented graphically in Fig. 3.2.

Two Critical Factors in Observational Learning

Bandura and Walters' distinction has been extended into an informational analysis of observational learning[16]. According to this view, a child does not just learn new behavior from watching others; he also learns when or whether it is appropriate to act or avoid acting in certain ways. In other words, he uses all of the information contained in what he has seen to decide upon his own action. Two factors — vicarious consequences and the status of the model — have been found to be particularly important in this process.

Vicarious Consequences

Vicarious consequences refer to outcomes which accrue to the model as a result of his behavior. When these outcomes are positive or desirable, they are called *vicarious rewards*; negative outcomes are called *vicarious punishments*.

In an important experiment, Bandura demonstrated the effects of vicarious consequences on acceptance of aggressive behavior[17]. He showed nursery school children a five-minute film on a television screen in which an adult demonstrated four novel aggressive responses against a large plastic Bobo doll. One-third of the children saw only the novel responses — they formed the no-consequence control group. Another third of the children saw an additional scene in which the model was generously rewarded with candy and other treats, and enthusiastically praised for his aggressive behavior. The remaining children saw the model both physically and verbally punished for aggression. Then each child was taken to a playroom containing among other toys, a plastic Bobo doll.

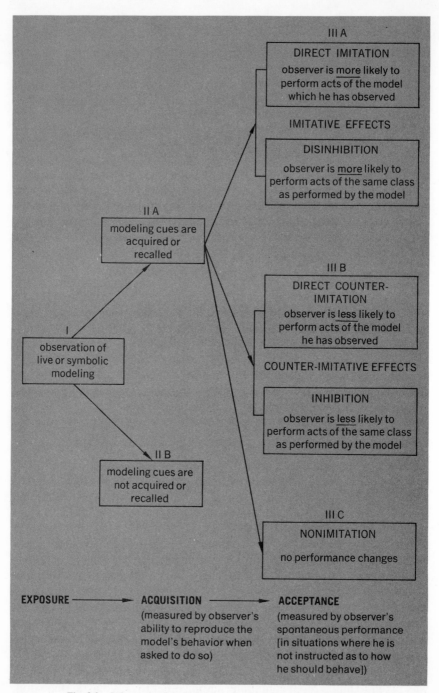

Fig. 3.2 Schematic of the steps involved in observational learning.

42

The measure of acceptance was the number of aggressive behaviors now spontaneously performed by the child.

Children who saw the model punished performed fewer aggressive responses than children in the other two experimental conditions. A measure of acquisition followed — an adult experimenter offered the child rewards for each of the model's responses he could reproduce. In this case, when the children were offered incentives for performing, all groups showed the same high level of learning. Children in the model-punished conditions clearly learned to aggress but apparently used the consequences to the model as an indication of what might happen to them if they acted in the same way, and prudently decided not to imitate. But, most important, they still retained these novel forms of aggression and were able and willing to use them later.

Status of the Model

The other major set of data related to an informational analysis of observational learning is concerned with observer-model characteristics. One is especially relevant to television and imitation: status of the model. Although many of the relevant studies employ live rather than symbolic modeling, they still offer information about the processes involved that are pertinent to our understanding of television's effects.

Several studies show that high status models are imitated more often than low status ones[18,19]. The high status model may be imitated because he or she is presumed to know what is appropriate or permissible behavior. Sometimes, the high status model is imitated simply because the observer aspires to high status himself and hopes to attain it by imitating behaviors of the high status model. Additional evidence offers support for the proposition that competence of the model is also an important variable for the amount of imitation[20,21,22].

Observational Learning: Implications of Basic Research for Understanding TV's Effects

Network officials have sometimes justified television violence because the "bad guy" is always punished for his behavior. The usual sequence involves aggression by the villain, through which he achieves his immediate objectives (the plans for the latest nuclear weapon, or the contents of the bank vault). Then the hero catches up with and punishes the villain — by shooting, beating, or otherwise physically assaulting him. The hero then walks off with a promotion, a blond, a bottle of champagne, or, if he is lucky, all three plus a vacation in the sun. The observer is thus exposed to *two* aggressive models: one punished and the other rewarded. Research suggests that the child will learn the aggressive behavior of both characters. But, because of the different consequences, the actions of the rewarded model might easily be copied immediately, while the actions of the punished model will not be. Still, the child may later display the behavior he has learned from the punished model if the incentives become sufficient; for example, when peers encourage it. Research on model characteristics suggests that television content is especially conducive to observational learning. We saw in Chapter 2 that high status aggressive models, those most likely to be imitated, make up the greatest proportion of the television population.

Thus, it is easy to see that children might react to televised aggression by becoming more aggressive themselves. But another alternative must be considered: can viewing violence actually reduce the likelihood of aggressive behavior?

THE CATHARSIS HYPOTHESIS

Many centuries before television aggression became a subject for public concern and controversy, Aristotle speculated about the psychological effects of drama, suggesting that by witnessing dramatic offerings the audience "purges" its feelings of grief, fear, and pity. Since then the same idea has been extended to feelings of aggression and anger. The basic notion is that frustration (for example, not getting one's way), being insulted, and the like, produce an increase in aggressive drive. Increased drive is unpleasant and the individual seeks to reduce it through aggressive acts. But, according to the catharsis hypothesis, the drive may also be reduced by fantasy aggression. The original catharsis hypothesis simply predicted that viewing violence would reduce aggression in the observer[23]. Despite some limited support in studies with college students, this hypothesis was rejected in a number of investigations with children[24,25].

In a study by Alberta Siegel[25], for example, pairs of nursery school children were taken to an experimental room, where they saw a film. Then the experimenter left the room, and the children played and were observed for a 14-minute period. Play with aggressive toys (e.g., toy daggers) as well as outright assault on each other were recorded. Each pair of children saw both an aggressive film (a Woody Woodpecker cartoon) and a nonaggressive film (about the Little Red Hen) about one week apart. If the catharsis hypothesis were correct, the children should have been *less* aggressive after viewing the violent cartoon. In fact, they were actually somewhat *more* aggressive after watching it than after viewing the non-aggressive film. This has been the usual result, but the catharsis hypothesis was not discarded entirely.

Seymour Feshbach and Robert Singer have presented a modified formulation of the catharsis hypothesis[26]. They suggest that the mass media serve to stimulate fantasy and that the fantasy thus provided must satisfy some sort of need. In this view, fantasies can be seen as . . .

> . . . *substitutes for overt behavior which are partly rewarding in themselves and which may reduce arousal, as coping or adaptive mechanisms useful when delays in gratification occur, and as aids to arousal possibly culminating in overt behavior.* (p. 11)

According to Feshbach and Singer, fantasy may act to reduce aggression in one of several ways. It may, for example, reduce the arousal level of an angry individual: If he can sufficiently punish his nagging mother-in-law or demanding boss in his thoughts, he will feel less desire to punish them in his actions. Or, if the individual is rewarded often enough for fantasy aggression (he pushes his boss off a bridge in thought and feels better afterward) he gets into the habit of using fantasy aggression to "cathart" (drain off) his aggressive feelings with the result that he is *less* likely to actually behave aggressively. Television, according to this view, can provide fantasy material usable to the viewer for catharsis, especially if he perceives the circumstances and the characters as similar to himself and his own victims.

Another way in which televised violence might reduce aggression is through inhibition.

> *It may frighten the viewer of violence and its possible consequences; it may create over aggressive impulses and the eventuality that they may be acted out. The viewer consequently avoids aggressive behavior in order to reduce his fear of what he may do or what may be done to him.* (p. 15)

The Feshbach and Singer Experiment: A Field Study of Catharsis

In the late 1960s Feshbach and Singer performed an ambitious test of their revised catharsis hypothesis, investigating the effects of television violence on a large number of boys in the natural environment[26]. The subjects were approximately 400 adolescent and preadolescent boys in institutional settings in New York and California. Three of the institutions were private schools, drawing on upper middle-class youngsters. The remaining four were homes for boys who lacked adequate home care or were experiencing social and personal adjustment difficulties. These latter children were of predominantly lower-class background; 35% were black and an additional 10% were Chicano or Puerto Rican.

The boys were divided into two groups, according to whether they watched aggressive or nonaggressive television. Each boy was required to watch at least 6 hours of televison per week for 6 weeks; he could watch more if he wished, but all programs had to be from a designated list. The aggressive diet consisted of about 75 programs, of which 20 were seen most frequently (e.g., *Bonanza*, *I Spy*, *Rifleman*, and *The Untouchables*). The nonaggressive diet consisted of about 150 programs, with about 50 being viewed relatively frequently (e.g., *Andy Williams*, *Gomer Pyle*, *Petticoat Junction*, and *Wide World of Sports*).

A number of measures of aggression were employed, including projective tests and attitude questionnaires. The most important measure, however, concerning the effects of television violence on aggressive *behavior*, was the behavior rating scale. This scale consisted of 26 items, 19 of which pertained to aggression. Five items referred to physical aggression toward others, self, or property. The remainder referred to nonphysical aggression including grumbling, being bossy, sullen, or disobedient, as well as cursing or arguing angrily. Each behavior was rated once a day according to whether it was directed toward authority or toward peers, whether it was provoked or unprovoked, and whether it was mild or moderately strong. The raters were house parents, supervisors, teachers, and proctors.

Feshbach and Singer found that, on the behavior rating scale, boys in the nonaggressive TV group were more aggressive than boys in the aggressive content group, both in aggression toward peers and in aggression toward authority. When the data were analyzed by institutions, this difference was found to be due solely to three of the seven institutions — all boys' homes. Here, then, aggression was less frequent among those on the aggressive TV diet, as predicted by the catharsis hypothesis. On a week-by-week basis aggression in boys in the nonaggressive TV group increased over the 7 weeks in which data were gathered; that of boys in the aggressive TV group declined over the same period.

In the private schools, the reverse pattern appeared: boys in the nonaggressive TV groups declined significantly in aggression, and boys in the aggressive television group tended to increase. This suggested that *dis-*

inhibition was at work, with violence viewing making some boys more aggressive; but when the two groups were compared, the differences were not significant.

While these findings provide some support for the catharsis hypothesis, the study is subject to a number of criticisms[27]. A particularly important problem concerns differential liking of the programs viewed by control and experimental subjects. Based on the data presented by Feshbach and Singer, Chaffee and McLeod[28] showed that boys in the nonaggressive TV group liked their assigned programs significantly *less* than boys in the aggressive television group. Thus, an important alternative explanation — or rival hypothesis — for the fact that some control subjects were more aggressive is that they resented being restricted to nonaggressive programs, and this resentment was expressed in an increase in aggression.

Another difficulty relates to the experimental treatments themselves. A crucial requirement of experimental studies is that all groups be treated identically except for the manipulation of the independent variable. Unfortunately, the Feshbach and Singer study did not meet this requirement. Boys in the nonaggressive TV group in institutions where the catharsis effect appeared had objected strongly to not being permitted to watch *Batman* (a highly aggressive program); the investigators then permitted them to include *Batman* in their list. This procedure constitutes an important difference in the treatment of the groups. Yielding to "a very strong objection" may very well have encouraged such related actions as grumbling, complaining, breaking rules, becoming sullen, refusing tasks, or acting bossy in other matters (all of which were scored as aggressive behaviors on the rating scale). Thus, another important rival hypothesis is that experimental differences may have resulted from subjects having won an unreasonable demand from experimenters in one group and not in the other, rather than from differences in the television diet *per se*.

An Attempt to Repeat the Feshbach and Singer Experiment

One way to determine whether or not problems such as the foregoing actually did produce false support for the catharsis hypothesis is to perform a similar experiment in which the problems are eliminated. Wells performed just such a replication[29]. He found that boys who watched only television fare from which all "action and adventure had been expunged" were somewhat more aggressive *verbally* than those who watched a heavy diet of aggression. But he reports, from various other lines of evidence, "that the greater verbal aggression [from this group] may have come from complaints about the 'lousy' shows they were required to watch...". His other results, and an interpretation of them, were presented this way by the Surgeon General's Advisory Committee on Television and Social Behavior[30]:

> ...in a direct reversal of Feshbach and Singer—Wells found significantly greater physical aggressiveness among boys who viewed the more violent television programs....the differences... were limited to boys who were above average in aggression before the study began....[Wells] interprets the greater physical aggression elicited by the more violent program diet as a tendency for the action-adventure content to stimulate aggressive behavior. He found no evidence [in this replication of Feshbach and Singer] that would support a catharsis interpretation, unless the differences in regard to verbal aggressiveness were so interpreted. (p. 66, emphasis added)

Recently, two additional experiments have been performed in a field setting to test the catharsis hypothesis further. Again, as in the Wells' study, no evidence for catharsis was found in naturally occurring aggressive behavior; instead, exposure to entertainment violence instigated more aggression than was found among boys who watched non-aggressive fare[31].

The evidence, then, gives little support for the idea that observing violence drains off aggressive impulses, making observers *less* likely to be violent. Indeed, the data suggest a possibility directly opposite to the catharsis hypothesis—that watching aggression may have an instigating effect on the observer, making him *more* likely to be aggressive. In the next two chapters we will examine further evidence which gives strong support for the hypothesis that viewing violence increases aggression.

REFERENCES

1. Schramm, W., Lyle, J., & Parker, E. B. *Television in the lives of our children.* Stanford, California: Stanford University Press, 1961.
2. Merriam, E. We're teaching our children that violence is fun. *The Ladies' Home Journal,* October, 1964. (Down Publishing, Inc. Used by permission of *Ladies' Home Journal.*) Reprinted in O. N. Larsen (ed.). *Violence and the mass media.* New York: Harper & Row, 1968.
3. Wertham, F. School for violence. *The New York Times,* July 5, 1964. (© 1964 by The

New York Times Company. Reprinted by permission.) Reprinted in O. N. Larsen (ed.). *Violence and the mass media.* New York: Harper & Row, 1968.
4. Larsen, O. N., Gray, L. N., & Fortis, J. G. Goals and goal-achievement methods in television content: Models for anomie? *Sociological Inquiry,* 1963, **8**, 180–196.
5. Himmelweit, H., Oppenheim, A. N., & Vince, P. *Television and the child: An empirical study of the effects of television on the young.* London: Oxford University Press, 1958.
6. Gerbner, G. Violence in television drama: Trends and symbolic functions. In G. A. Comstock and E. A. Rubinstein (eds.). *Television and social behavior. Vol. I: Media content and control.* Washington, D.C.: U.S. Government Printing Office, 1972, pp. 28–187.
7. Rabinovitch, M. S., McLean, M. S., Jr., Markham, J. W., & Talbott, A. D. Children's violence perception as a function of television violence. In G. A. Comstock, E. A. Rubinstein, and J. P. Murray (eds.). *Television and social behavior. Vol. V.: Television's Effects: Further explorations.* Washington, D.C.: U.S. Government Printing Office, 1972, pp. 231–252.
8. Rosenhan, D. & White, G. M. Observation and rehearsal as determinants of pro-social behavior. *Journal of Personality and Social Psychology,* 1967, **5**, 424–431.
9. Bandura, A. & Mischel, W. Modification of self-imposed delay of reward through exposure to live and symbolic models. *Journal of Personality and Social Psychology,* 1965, **2**, 698–705.
10. Liebert, R. M., Odom, R. D., Hill, J. H., & Huff, R. L. Effects of age and rule familiarity on the production of modeled language constructions. *Developmental Psychology,* 1969, **1**, 108–112,
11. Coates, B. & Hartup, W. Age and verbalization in observational learning. *Developmental Psychology,* 1969, **1**, 556–562.
12. Bryan, J. & Walbeck, N. Preaching and practicing generosity: Children's actions and reactions. *Child Development,* 1970, **41**, 329–353.
13. Bandura, A. & Menlove, F. L. Factors determining vicarious extinction of avoidance behavior through symbolic modeling. *Journal of Personality and Social Psychology,* 1967, **5**, 16–22.
14. Hill, J. H., Liebert, R. M., & Mott, D. E. Vicarious extinction of avoidance behavior through films: An initial test. *Psychological Reports,* 1968, **22**, 192.
15. Bandura, A. & Walters, R. H. *Social learning and personality development.* New York: Holt, Rinehart & Winston, 1963.
16. Liebert, R. M. & Fernandez, L. E. Imitation as a function of vicarious and direct reward. *Developmental Psychology,* 1970, **2**, 230–232.
17. Bandura, A. Influence of models' reinforcement contingencies on the acquisition of imitative responses. *Journal of Personality and Social Psychology,* 1965, **1**, 589–595.
18. Lefkowitz, N. M., Blake, R. R., & Mouton, J. S. Status factors in pedestrian violation of traffic signals. *Journal of Abnormal and Social Psychology,* 1955, **51**, 704–706.
19. Harvey, O. J. & Rutherford, J. Status in the informal group: Influence and influencibility at differing age levels. *Child Development,* 1960, **31**, 377–385.
20. Hammer, M. A. The effects of model exposure, status, and task competence on imitative behavior. *Dissertation Abstracts,* 1971, **31**, 6158–6159.
21. Schuh, J. V. The effect of adult model nurturance and competence on preschool children's imitative behavior. *Dissertation Abstracts,* 1971, **31**, 6245.
22. Britt, D. W. Effects of probability of reinforcement and social stimulus consistency on imitation. *Journal of Personality and Social Psychology,* 1971, **18**, 189–200.

23. Feshbach, S. The drive-reducing function of fantasy behavior. *Journal of Abnormal and Social Psychology*, 1955, **50**, 3–11.
24. Mussen, P. & Rutherford, E. Effects of aggressive cartoons on children's aggressive play. *Journal of Abnormal and Social Psychology*, 1961, **62**, 461–464.
25. Siegel, A. E. Film-mediated fantasy aggression and strength of aggressive drive. *Child Development*, 1956, **27**, 365–378.
26. Feshbach, S. & Singer, R. *Television and aggression*. San Francisco: Jossey-Bass, 1971.
27. Liebert, R. M., Sobol, M. P., & Davidson, E. S. Catharsis of aggression among institutionalized boys: Fact or artifact? In G. A. Comstock, E. A. Rubinstein, and J. P. Murray (eds.), *Television and social behavior. Vol. V: Television's effects: Further explorations.* Washington, D.C.: U.S. Government Printing Office, 1972, pp. 351–358.
28. Chaffee, S. H. & McLeod, J. M. Adolescents, parents, and television violence. Paper presented at American Psychological Association meeting, Washington, D.C., September 1971.
29. Wells, W. D. Television and aggression: A replication of an experimental field study. University of Chicago, 1972. (Mimeographed abstract.)
30. Cisin, I. H., Coffin, T. E., Janis, I. L., Klapper, J. T., Mendelsohn, H., Omwake, E., Pinderhughes, C. A., Pool, I. de Sola, Siegel, A. E., Wallace, A. F. C., Watson, A. S., & Wiebe, G. O. *Television and growing up: The impact of televised violence*. Washington, D.C.: U.S. Government Printing Office, 1972.
31. Parke, R. D., Berkowitz, L., Leyens, J. P., West, S., & Sebastian, R. Movie violence and aggression: A field experimental approach. Unpublished manuscript, Fels Research Institute and University of Wisconsin, 1972.

4

TELEVISION AND AGGRESSION:
LABORATORY STUDIES

The Wells' experiment, and other findings discussed in Chapter 3, suggest that televised violence does not decrease and may actually increase aggressive behavior in youthful viewers. We will now consider that possibility in some detail, beginning in this chapter with the laboratory evidence and then turning, in the next, to field studies.

THE LABORATORY STRATEGY

The experiments described in this chapter were all conducted in a laboratory setting; special conditions were created to permit researchers to ask about certain relationships between violence viewing and aggressive behavior. At first appearance, this may seem a peculiar and artificial strategy.

Laboratory studies are *not* designed to approximate the natural environment. They are purposely conducted in an artificial environment to enable the researcher to explore important psychological processes precisely. Such a strategy parallels the development of a new type of aircraft by testing its wing shape and structural soundness in wind tunnels and heat chambers rather than haphazardly putting it together without testing to see if it will fly.

The laboratory strategy does immediately raise one persistent question, though it applies to nonlaboratory situations as well.

What Is Aggression?

Most people probably agree that aggression includes injury to another, but beyond that individual discrepancies appear. Even so, minor variations in each of our personal definitions of aggression are usually no problem in ordinary discourse. Scientists, however, require much more specific definitions than those offered by common usage.

Let us consider some definitions that social scientists have offered. An early one considered aggression as a response having for its goal the injury of a living organism[1]. Some, objecting to this definition because it involves purpose or intent, define aggression as "a response that delivers noxious stimuli to another organism"[2] (p. 3). Such a definition no longer focuses on the behavior of the aggressor; rather it assesses the consequences to the target. Thus stepping on someone's toe on the subway is aggression; shooting at and missing someone's head is not. Clearly, intent cannot be left out so easily, difficult as it is to assess. Effectiveness should not be the sole criterion — the rifle shot that misses and the karate chop which hits only air are aggressive, regardless of lack of results.

What about physical versus verbal aggression? Most of us would wish to include at least some kinds of verbal behavior as aggressive — angry insults or malicious gossip can clearly hurt the target, and often this is the intention of the speaker. Whether one wishes to include grumbling, complaining, and acting bossy, as Feshbach and Singer did, is another question[3]; these behaviors are annoying, but whether they are aggressive is a matter of opinion.

A final issue concerns fantasy and play aggression. Many psychologists and psychiatrists consider reactions to Rorschach ink blots and word association tests to be valid measures of aggression. Included in this class of responses are the play measures of aggression used by many researchers. Once again, whether these behaviors are to be considered as aggressive is a matter of both scientific and subjective judgment.

Most psychologists consider "aggression" to be a *theoretical construct*, a convenient way of talking about a lot of different behaviors which appear to be related. In any individual study, the investigator takes one behavior which he feels falls in the category of "aggression" and uses that as his definition. He may try to relate the behavior he is calling aggression to other behaviors; for example, relating a laboratory shock measure of aggression to real-life aggression by comparing the responses of violent prisoners to those of college students[4].

That this issue cannot ever be resolved entirely should not be permitted to obscure our search for TV's effects; there was a valid need in the studies discussed below to use many measures and encompass a broad sample of the meaning of aggression.

APPROACHING THE QUESTION

Through observational learning, violence viewing might make several distinct but related contributions to aggressive behavior; to examine them in turn we must recall the three step analysis of observational learning described and shown on pp. 41–42. As we saw, the first stage requires exposure to some form of modeled example. It is clear that violent television fare is available in overwhelming abundance and that children are exposed to it both frequently and regularly (*cf*. Chapter 2). So it is the second stage, learning or acquisition, that we must consider next.

Acquisition of Novel Aggressive Behavior from Television

No one would doubt that children can learn novel forms of behavior — both words and actions — from simply watching others. But it is only through systematic research under specially created conditions in the laboratory that we are able to see the degree to which this form of learning is mediated by television and to understand the underlying processes involved.

Many studies have been designed to determine whether brief exposure to novel forms of aggression on television will lead to their acquisition by young children. The answer has been clear and uniform: television's influence is indeed potent. In one such study, for example, some children saw a simulated television program in which an adult behaved in unusual, novel, and aggressive ways against a large Bobo doll, including kicking and hitting the play victim with a large mallet while accompanied by her own hostile, *Batman*-like verbalizations (*Pow . . . Socko*). Other children saw a similar performance, but with a cartoon format. The examples, then, permit us to speak about both familiar human and unrealistic animal characters (in this case the newly created figure, *Herman the Cat*). Observations of the children while they played later left little doubt that most had learned to act in new, aggressive ways. The appearance of these types of behaviors (and other aggressive actions as well) was now much more frequent in the TV groups than in the control group who did not observe modeled aggression[5].

Particularly striking in these studies is the degree to which some of the children appear to become virtual "carbon copies" of the aggressive models whom they have seen on a television console. Photographs illustrating some of the effects, which occur for preschool children of both sexes, are shown in Fig. 4.1. The topmost frames show the model's performance of four novel aggressive responses while the middle and bottom frames respectively depict a boy and girl spontaneously reproducing what they had seen earlier "on TV."

But the effects shown in these early studies spanned only a short time interval. In the usual circumstances outside the laboratory new learning may be important only if it can be retained for some length of time. Can a single exposure to television have such a long-term influence? Two studies by David Hicks have disclosed that the answer is "Yes."

Hicks showed preschool children simulated television programs with aggressive content, similar to the ones used in earlier studies. After determining the degree of immediate learning which had occurred, a long time interval was permitted to pass: 6 months in one study[6] and 8 months in another[7]. Remarkably, despite this long delay (the children had never seen the program again or had any kind of "reminder" regarding its contents), the ability to perform the new forms of aggression was retained by the youngsters. About 40% of the TV model's hostile acts could still be reproduced — after a single showing of less than 10 minutes, seen 8 months previously!

Acceptance

Direct Imitative Effects

Despite the fact that children learn and retain new aggressive behaviors from television, we might wonder how likely they are to ever perform them unless, of course, we actually ask them to do so. The data suggest quite convincingly, though, that spontaneous imitation of aggressive behaviors learned from television does occur. This is confirmed by laboratory studies, documented case histories, and reports of the youngsters themselves.

When Lyle and Hoffman asked first-graders whether they had ever copied what they had seen on television, more than 60% said they had done so; when asked to indicate the *type* of program that they imitated, adventure shows (such as *Batman*) led the list. The children did not usually act out these aggressive acts alone; most used televised aggression as a guide for their own actions when playing with friends[8].

Case studies, too, have shown that aggressive and antisocial behaviors are learned from television; the boy who put ground glass in the family dinner and the proliferation of better techniques for hijacking airplanes

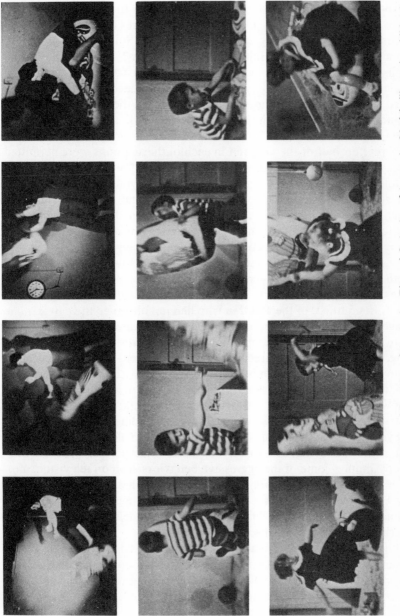

Fig. 4.1 Photographs from the film *Social Learning of Aggression Through Imitation of Aggressive Models*, illustrating children's acquisition of aggressive responses through observational learning (Source: Courtesy of Dr. Albert Bandura).

(*see* pp. 1–3) illustrate an imitative process which parallels the one studied in the laboratory.

Experimental evidence for television's potential to induce direct imitation of aggression is provided very clearly in a series of recent studies. In the first of these, 4- and 5-year-old boys from a Sunday school kindergarten served as subjects. Half of them observed a $2\frac{1}{2}$-minute color sound film in which an adult male model aggressed against a human clown. The behavior displayed by this symbolic model included sharp and unprovoked verbal insults to the clown, shooting at the clown with a toy machine gun, and beating the clown vigorously with a plastic mallet. The others saw no such film[9].

Thereafter, half of the children in each of these groups were permitted to play in a room where they found a human clown standing idly by, as well as a mallet and a toy gun. The remaining youngsters were placed in a comparable situation, except that they found a plastic Bobo doll rather than a human. The children were left in this situation for 10 minutes, during which time their aggressive responses toward the clown, plastic or human, were recorded. Not surprisingly, the brief film did increase aggression against the inflated Bobo. However, regardless of whether the children had seen the aggressive film or not, the majority of those who were placed with the plastic toy exhibited some aggressive action. In contrast, of the children who had not observed the movie, none engaged in any sort of aggressive behavior toward the human clown. There are, of course, strong inhibitions against aggressing toward a human being, even one who is attired as a clown, and there was no provocation for doing so. Nonetheless, observation of the aggressive movie did lead to imitative physical assaults against the human clown, including at least one swat with the mallet which was hard enough that the victim showed a red mark on her arm several hours later. The basic finding has been replicated with youngsters from a rural background[10] and with older children[11].

In sum, the evidence strongly suggests that normal children may directly imitate some of the aggressive behaviors seen on television. Yet, in our experience, many parents are surprised at these findings. After all, they are frequently present when their children are exposed to televised violence and often are not able to discern any modeling effects. A recent experiment suggests why this is so.

Children were exposed to an aggressive model and then allowed to play in one of three different situations: in the presence of adults, in the presence of peers, and alone[12]. The general pattern of results disclosed that *the presence of an adult reduced the amount of aggression* but that the presence of a *same-sexed peer* increased aggression, relative to the control group. Thus, in life situations, the effects of aggressive modeling may occur most often under circumstances where they cannot be observed by parents or other adults. Another researcher citing earlier studies, reached a similar conclusion[13]:

> ...*parental evaluation or instruction regarding the permissibility of aggression seen in the media can be effective in controlling aggression imitation, but this communication may be irrelevant when adults are not later present to monitor the child's behavior.* (p. 403)

Inhibitory and Disinhibitory Effects

We cannot usually, for the sake of research, place children in situations where they would be capable of directly imitating the violence that is seen daily on commercial television. Many violent incidents on television involve the use of weapons; many result in severe injury or death. Obviously no responsible investigator would place a child in a playroom with another child and a real gun to see if viewing aggressive films increases the number of shootings. In addition to the ethical difficulties, direct imitation requires a circumstance virtually identical to the one observed. But since real-life circumstances rarely mirror those of television, inhibitory and disinhibitory influences are more important from a social perspective. Therefore, much recent research focuses on them.

Aggressive Play

In a relatively early study, nursery school children's aggressive play increased after viewing an aggressive film[14]. Half the subjects saw one cartoon figure aggress against another by hitting, biting, and so on, for virtually the entire duration of the film. Another group of children saw a film of a mother bear and three baby bears playing together. Each child was then presented with two toys and his play observed. Pushing a lever on one toy caused one doll to turn and hit another doll over the head with a stick. Depressing the lever on the other toy caused a wooden ball, enclosed in a cage, to jump through obstacles. The toys were presented side by side; the child could operate either or both at once if he wished. Children who were exposed to the aggressive film used the hitting doll toy more often than those who watched the nonaggressive film. Thus, at least at the level of play, disinhibition occurred.

In view of the fact that most television programs appear to depict aggression as a potent technique for power and achievement, investigations which have focused upon the inhibiting and disinhibiting effects of consequences accruing to a model for aggression are of particular importance. In one such study, Bandura, Ross, and Ross exposed one group of nursery school boys and girls to a television program in which one character, Johnny, refuses another, Rocky, the opportunity to play with some toys. The program goes on to show a series of aggressive responses by Rocky, including hitting Johnny with a rubber ball, shooting darts at Johnny's cars, hitting Johnny with a baton, lassoing him with a hula-hoop, and so on. At the end of this sequence, Rocky, the aggressor, is playing with all of Johnny's toys, treating himself to sweet beverages and cookies, and finally departs with Johnny's hobby horse under his arm and a sack of Johnny's toys over his shoulder. At this point, a commentator announces that Rocky was victorious. In a second group, the program was rearranged so that after Rocky's initial aggression, Johnny retaliated in kind by administering a sound thrashing to the aggressor[15].

Two other groups served as controls; in one, a nonaggressive but highly expressive television program was observed, and in the second no television program was seen. Children's subsequent aggressive responses while playing for 20 minutes in a special test room constituted the primary dependent measure. The results clearly showed that those who observed a rewarded aggressor showed far more aggression themselves than children in the other groups. Moreover, at the conclusion of the experiment the children were asked to state which of the characters, Rocky or Johnny, they would prefer to emulate. Sixty percent of those who observed Rocky rewarded for his behavior indicated that they would select him as a model; only 20% of those who saw him punished indicated that they would choose to emulate him. Additionally, the authors noted a classic example of how socially reprehensible but successful modeled aggressive acts may influence children. One of the girls, who had expressed marked disapproval of Rocky's aggressive behavior as it occurred, later exhibited many of his aggressive responses. Finally, in an apparent effort to make her emulation of the ruthless but successful Rocky complete, she turned to the experimenter and inquired, "Do you have a sack here?"

A number of other studies have also used aggressive play as a measure of aggression; all found that subjects who viewed an aggressive film model engaged in more aggressive play than children who were not so exposed[16,17,18,19].

Direct Physical Discomfort

Increases in aggressive play suggest a general disinh
do not define the social implications of the effect. So, to ue.
viewing aggression will actually make young observers more likely .
inflict physical discomfort on others, alternative measures of aggression
have also been used. In one study, hospital attendants, high school boys,
and young women viewed either the knife-fight scene from *Rebel Without
a Cause* or a film of adolescents engaging in constructive activities[20]. Both
before and after viewing the film, everyone participated in an experiment
which ostensibly required shocking another person for making errors on a
learning test. The dependent measure was the difference in the intensity of
shocks given during the two sessions. In all three groups, those who saw
the aggressive film gave stronger shocks in the second session than did
those who saw the constructive film.

This particular measure has been used in many other investigations which demonstrate both that viewing violence increases aggression[21, 22, 23, 24], and that laboratory shock is related to real-life violence. In
one study, delinquent adolescent boys were either angered or treated
neutrally and then shown one of three films, two of which were aggressive
in content. Regardless of whether they were angered or not, seeing an
aggressive film produced more subsequent aggression (ostensible electric
shocks to another person) than did the neutral film. At the same time,
boys with a past history of aggressive behavior were more aggressive than
other boys[25]. In a second study, comparing the effects of aggressive and
nonaggressive live models, male college students and young male in-
mates in a maximum security prison for violent criminals participated.
Again, in both groups, those exposed to an aggressive model administered
stronger shocks than those exposed to a nonaggressive model. Further,
the prisoners were more aggressive than the college students, demonstrating the relationship between the laboratory measure and real-life
aggression[4].

A similar result has been found in a study of younger children[26]. The
participants, 136 boys and girls between the ages of 5 and 9, were taken to
a room containing a television monitor, and told that they could watch
television for a few minutes, until the experimenter was ready. The
sequences they saw came from actual television shows, but had been
videotaped earlier. For all the children, the first 2 minutes of film consisted
of commercials selected for their humor and attention-getting characteristics. The following $3\frac{1}{2}$ minutes constituted the experimental treatment.

ialf the children viewed a sequence from *The Untouchables* which contained a chase, two fistfighting scenes, two shootings, and a knifing. The other children saw an exciting sports sequence. For everyone, the final minute seen was another commercial.

Each child was then escorted to another room and seated in front of a large box which had wires leading into the next room. On the box were a green button, labeled HELP, and a red button, labeled HURT. Over the two buttons was a white light. The experimenter explained that the wires were connected to a game that another child in the adjoining room was going to play. The game involved turning a handle, and each time the child started to turn the handle the white light would come on. The experimenter explained that by pushing the buttons the subject could either help the other child by making the handle easier to turn or hurt the other child by making the handle hot. The longer he pushed the buttons, the more he helped or hurt the other child. He was further told that he had to push one of the buttons every time the light came on. After insuring that the child understood which button was which, the experimenter left the room and the light came on 20 times. After this, each child was taken to a

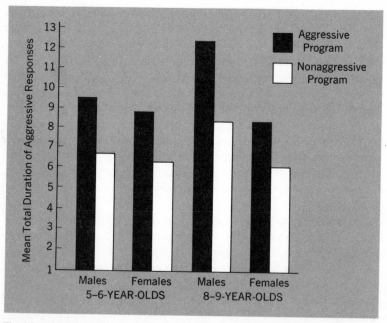

Fig. 4.2   Mean total duration of aggressive responses (Source: Liebert and Baron[26]).

playroom containing aggressive and nonaggressive toys and aggressive play was assessed.

Using total duration of pushing the HURT button as their measure of aggression, the investigators found that children who viewed the aggressive program were significantly more willing to hurt another child than were those who watched the sports sequence. When average duration was computed (total duration divided by the number of HURT responses), the same results were obtained. As seen in Fig. 4.2, the pattern appears for boys and girls of both ages.

It was possible that children who viewed the violent television scene pushed the HURT button longer because they were more excited or aroused. If this line of reasoning is correct *any* response of this group would be of higher intensity; therefore, they also should have pushed the HELP button longer. They did not. The programs used made no difference in total duration, average duration or number of HELP responses. Thus, the differences obtained can be confidently attributed to an instigating effect of viewing violence. Consistent with previous research, children in the aggressive film condition also were more aggressive in the play situation, with the effects much stronger for younger boys than for any of the other groups.

Justification for Aggression in TV Violence: Does it Matter?

Clearly there is a great deal of evidence that televised aggression can disinhibit young viewers so that they become more likely to behave aggressively. But the TV programs seen have often been either simulated or taken out of context. If youngsters see entire programs, with violence justified according to a regular story line, will disinhibition still occur?

It is known that factors such as provocation and justification in entertainment with aggressive content may alter the effects of that entertainment on adults. In one study, for example, college students were either insulted or not insulted and then (within each group) half of them viewed a film showing justified aggression while the other half saw a film showing unjustified aggression. Finally, they had an opportunity to shock the experimental confederate — the very one who had insulted them. These young men were most likely to give a large number of shocks, and shocks of long duration, if they had been angered and then seen entertainment in which justified aggression was depicted[27].

Another investigator has examined some of the factors which influence justification[28]. College men were angered, not by insulting them but by having an experimental confederate give them a large number of electric shocks in a learning experiment. The young men next saw a film clip of a fight scene. In one condition, the justification was based on vengeance; the victor was seen as avenging an unfair beating which he had previously received. In a second condition, justification was based on self-defense. In a third situation, the introduction to the film combined both vengeance and self-defense motives. In the fourth condition, no introduction and thus no justification was provided at all. Then the roles were reversed: the students had the opportunity to shock the experimental confederate. In terms of number and duration of shocks given to the confederate, those in the fourth (no justification) condition were lowest in level of aggression; students in the third (vengeance and self-defense) condition were the highest.

We can now relate these findings to television violence content. Violence by the villain, which is usually punished, is seen as unjustified. However, violence by the hero is usually seen as justified either for reasons of vengeance or self-defense or both. Such justifications appear to make violent heroes uniquely inviting models for emulation by adolescents.

A Study With Children

Aimée Leifer and Donald Roberts investigated the effects of the motivation for and consequences of televised violence on children's aggression[29]. Previous studies of justification had usually employed college students, not young children. Additionally, earlier justification studies and the response consequences studies used relatively short films, in which motivations and/or consequences were closely related, especially in time, to the action in the film. But television programs usually last a half hour or more; the motivations of the characters are less explicitly stated, and consequences to the aggressor may occur long after the aggressive acts themselves. Thus, Leifer and Roberts wished to investigate young children's understanding of these two factors in regular programming and their influence on children's attitudes toward violence. To do so they developed a measure of aggression based on the concept of the *response hierarchy.*

When an individual has a number of responses available to him, his alternatives are arranged in a hierarchy — a steplike progression from most probable to least probable. For example, in a threatening situation a very timid individual may prefer to run away. If he is unable to do so, his next choice may be to call for assistance. If this, too, is impossible he may attempt to placate the threatening party. Only as a last resort will he attack. In other words, if the first response is blocked, he will then try the second, and so on, until he has exhausted his repertoire of possible responses.

Leifer and Roberts suggest that the overt behavioral tests used in many studies tap only the first response in the hierarchy, but that the influence of television violence may be to change the relative positions of other responses as well. Televised violence may raise physical aggression from, say, the sixth most probable response to the second most probable response and thus increase the likelihood that aggression will occur.

Based on interviews with youngsters, these investigators developed 6 situations which were likely to anger younger children, aged 4–10, and 6 situations appropriate to older children and adolescents, aged 10–16. There were 4 characteristic types of responses—physical aggression, verbal aggression, escaping the situation, and positive coping (including telling an adult). A situation was presented and then the alternative responses were shown in such a way that each response was paired with every other response, giving a total of 6 pairs. These were presented to young children in a booklet; the child marked the picture depicting his chosen response. Older children saw the pictures on slides, and marked the letter "a" or "b" on an answer sheet. An example of a complete item, including the situation and the possible responses is shown in Fig. 4.3.

One study employing this measure involved 6 programs which had been assessed by adults in the community for amount of violence contained: 2 children's programs (*Rocket Robin Hood* and *Batman*), 2 westerns (*Rifleman*, and *Have Gun, Will Travel*), and 2 crime dramas (*Adam 12*, and *Felony Squad*). They were asked to list the violent episodes, the aggressor and victim in each incident, the victim's response, the justifiability of each act, and the appropriateness of immediate and final consequences. To ensure that the episodes were truly aggressive, the three most frequently listed ones were then used.

Participants were 271 youngsters in kindergarten, third-, sixth-, ninth-, and twelfth-grades. Each saw one of the programs, then filled out a multiple choice questionnaire, and finally the response hierarchy instrument. Further confirming a finding that is now familiar to us it was found that children who viewed the more aggressive programs were more likely to select physical aggression as a response. What was surprising, though, is that motivations, consequences, and the child's understanding of these factors were unrelated to subsequent aggressive responses. As the investigators themselves put it[29]:

Fig. 4.3   Sample of a complete response hierarchy item (Source: Leifer and Roberts[29]).

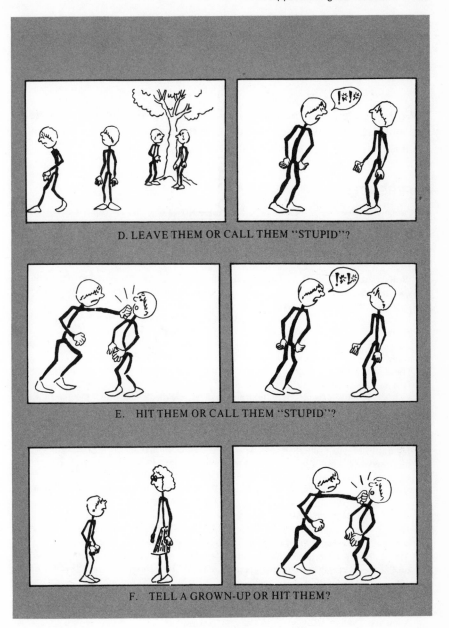

D. LEAVE THEM OR CALL THEM "STUPID"?

E.   HIT THEM OR CALL THEM "STUPID"?

F.   TELL A GROWN-UP OR HIT THEM?

Fig. 4.3 (cont'd)

Whatever analysis was performed, the amount of violence in the program affected the amount of aggression subsequently chosen. Nothing else about the program — the context within which violence was presented — seemed to influence subsequent aggression. (p. 89)

We have seen that the laboratory evidence is remarkably consistent, but must still ask whether the same pattern emerges when we turn to youngsters' free-ranging behavior in the natural environment.

REFERENCES

1. Dollard, J., Miller, N., Doob, L., Mowrer, O. H., & Sears, R. R. *Frustration and aggression.* New Haven: Yale University Press, 1939.
2. Buss, A. H. *The psychology of aggression.* New York: Wiley, 1961.
3. Feshbach, S. & Singer, R. *Television and aggression.* San Francisco: Jossey-Bass, 1971.
4. Wolf, B. M. & Baron, R. A. Is laboratory aggression related to aggression in naturalistic social situations? The influence of an aggressive model on the behavior of college student and prisoner observers. *Psychonomic Science*, 1971, **24**, 193–194.
5. Bandura, A., Ross, D., & Ross, S. A. Imitation of film-mediated aggressive models. *Journal of Abnormal and Social Psychology*, 1963, **66**, 3–11.
6. Hicks, D. J. Imitation and retention of film-mediated aggressive peer and adult models. *Journal of Personality and Social Psychology*, 1965, **2**, 97–100.
7. Hicks, D. J. Short- and long-term retention of affectively varied modeled behavior. *Psychonomic Science*, 1968, **11**, 369–370.
8. Lyle, J. & Hoffman, H. R. Children's use of television and other media. In E. A. Rubinstein, G. A. Comstock, and J. P. Murray (eds.). *Television and social behavior. Vol. IV: Television in day-to-day life: Patterns of use.* Washington, D.C.: U.S. Government Printing Office, 1972, pp. 129–256.
9. Hanratty, M. A., Liebert, R. M., Morris, L. W., & Fernandez, L. E. Imitation of film-mediated aggression against live and inanimate victims. *Proceedings of the 77th Annual Convention of the American Psychological Association*, 1969, 457–458.
10. Savitsky, J. C., Rogers, R. W., Izard, C. E., & Liebert, R. M. Role of frustration and anger in the imitation of filmed aggression against a human victim. *Psychological Reports*, 1971, **29**, 807–810.
11. Hanratty, M. A., O'Neal, E., & Sulzer, J. L. The effect of frustration upon imitation of aggression. *Journal of Personality and Social Psychology*, 1972, **21**, 30–34.
12. Martin, M. F., Gelfand, D. M., & Hartmann, D. P. Effects of adult and peer observers on children's responses to an aggressive model. *Child Development*, 1971, **42**, 1271–1275.
13. Goranson, R. E. A review of recent literature on psychological effects of media portrayals of violence. Report to the National Commission on the Causes and Prevention of Violence. 1969.
14. Lovaas, O. I. Effect of exposure to symbolic aggression on aggressive behavior. *Child Development*, 1961, **32**, 37–44.

15. Bandura, A., Ross, D., & Ross, S. A. Transmission of aggression through imitation of aggressive models. *Journal of Abnormal and Social Psychology*, 1961, **63**, 575–582.
16. Hartmann, D. P. & Gelfand, D. M. Motivational variables affecting performance of vicariously learned responses. Paper presented at Western Psychological Association Meeting, Vancouver, British Columbia, June 1969.
17. Nelson, J. P., Gelfand, D. M., & Hartmann, D. P. Children's aggression following competititon and exposure to an aggressive model. *Child Development*, 1969, **40**, 1085–1097.
18. Rosekrans, M. A. & Hartup, W. W. Imitative influences of consistent and inconsistent response consequences to a model on aggressive behavior in children. *Journal of Personality and Social Psychology*, 1967, **7**, 429–434.
19. Walters, R. H. & Willows, D. C. Imitative behavior of disturbed and nondisturbed children following exposure to aggressive and nonaggressive models. *Child Development*, 1968, **39**, 79–89.
20. Walters, R. H. & Llewellyn-Thomas, E. Enhancement of punitiveness by visual and audiovisual displays. *Canadian Journal of Psychology*, 1963, **17**, 244–255.
21. Berkowitz, L. & Geen, R. G. Film violence and the cue properties of available targets. *Journal of Personality and Social Psychology*, 1966, **3**, 525–530.
22. Berkowitz, L. & Geen, R. G. Stimulus qualities of the target of aggression: A further study. *Journal of Personality and Social Psychology*, 1967, **5**, 364–368.
23. Geen, R. G. & Berkowitz, L. Name-mediating aggressive cue properties. *Journal of Personality*, 1966, **34**, 456–465.
24. Geen, R. G. & Berkowitz, L. Some conditions facilitating the occurrence of aggression after the observation of violence. *Journal of Personality*, 1967, **35**, 666–676.
25. Hartmann, D. P. Influence of symbolically modelled instrumental aggression and pain cues on aggressive behavior. *Journal of Personality and Social Psychology*, 1969, **11**, 280–288.
26. Liebert, R. M. & Baron, R. A. Short-term effects of televised aggression on children's aggressive behavior. In J. P. Murray, E. A. Rubinstein, and G. A. Comstock (eds.). *Television and social behavior. Vol. II: Television and social learning.* Washington, D.C.: U.S. Government Printing Office, 1972, pp. 181–201.
27. Berkowitz, L. Some aspects of observed aggression. *Journal of Personality and Social Psychology*, 1965, **2**, 359–369.
28. Hoyt, J. L. Effect of media violence "justification" on aggression. *Journal of Broadcasting*, 1970, **14**, 455–465.
29. Leifer, A. & Roberts, D. Children's responses to television violence. In J. P. Murray, E. A. Rubinstein, and G. A. Comstock (eds.). *Television and social behavior. Vol. II: Television and social learning.* Washington, D.C.: U.S. Government Printing office, 1972, pp. 43–180.

5

TELEVISION AND AGGRESSION: FIELD STUDIES

Laboratory studies have greatly furthered our understanding of the relationship between exposure to televised violence and aggressive behavior by the young. We have seen demonstrations that children learn, and then often use, novel acts they have observed on television and in television-like formats, and that televised violence can also exercise a disinhibitory effect over many responses that can be thought of as aggressive. Laboratory studies have shown repeatedly and consistently that observing television violence can make children more willing to hurt others, more aggressive in their play, and more likely to select aggression as a preferred response in conflict situations.

In scientific discourse these findings would be viewed as strong evidence for a cause-effect relationship. But more is at stake here. We are dealing with a problem of great social significance, and must be certain that the causal relationship disclosed in laboratory studies can be generalized to the living rooms, televisions, and children of our society. Critics argue that the laboratory study alone cannot provide this certainty[1,2,3].

LIMITATIONS OF LABORATORY STUDIES

The laboratory experiment *is* limited in terms of the type of information it provides. As we have seen, television viewing is a frequent activity for most people, children and adults. But many spend at least some of their "television time" engaging in other activities; they talk, they read, they journey to the refrigerator. This is certainly not the case in most laboratory studies; the subject either watches alone or with an experimenter who is nonresponsive. He probably sits glued to the set, without the reactions or interruptions which are so much a part of daily viewing. One must bear these differences in mind; perhaps, critics have argued, the impact of television would be much less in a nonlaboratory setting.

Somewhat related to the differences in viewing conditions is the amount of time spent viewing. Most people watch 2 or 3 hours a day, often in a single sitting. Laboratory studies, in contrast, usually involve only about 10–30 minutes of television, sometimes less, and may not produce the same type of effects that occur when an individual watches for several hours at a time. Likewise, most studies involve only one session (if they involve two, one is usually devoted to testing rather than television watching); these studies may not apply to the effects of viewing day after day for many hours.

A related problem might also limit our certainty that television can instigate aggressive behavior in the real world. It has been argued, for example, that in those investigations in which the subject is capable (he thinks) of injuring another person, he may assume that no serious harm can result to his victim. An older subject might say: "After all, this is a scientific investigation in which the well-being of all of the participants will be safeguarded." (By the same argument, no retaliation would be expected.) Under these circumstances, in which aggression is relatively tolerated and approved, and the ultimate responsibility is the experimenter's, the subject may feel free of restraints and inhibitions which would be active in a naturalistic situation.

One critic summed up many of these issues as follows[3]:

> *Perhaps the major criticism of these studies is their artificiality. They smell of the laboratory and involve complex sequences of procedures that simply seem too far removed from the ordinary course of events in real life.* (p. 47)

In other words, if we are to take a conservative tack, we know from laboratory studies what type of relationship *can* exist between television violence and aggression, but cannot be wholly certain that this relationship *does* exist in the complex world of free-ranging behavior.

THE FIELD STUDY APPROACH

Field studies solve many of the problems inherent in laboratory research. They do not suffer from restrictions in viewing time, artificial viewing situations and, of particular importance, they can employ measures of aggression which almost all investigators would agree are relevant. There are two major types of field studies: correlational and experimental. In correlational studies, naturally occurring events are simply measured; in experimental studies, some aspect of a youngster's television diet is actually controlled.

ANSWERING QUESTIONS ABOUT TELEVISION: THE CORRELATIONAL METHOD

The correlational method is employed to determine if two (or more) variables are related; that is, to see if they change or co-vary together. Many social scientific research questions have been answered using this method. For example, "Is mental illness related to social class?" or, "Are grades related to IQ test scores?" The first step in applying the correlational method involves obtaining pairs of observations on a group of people. Next, the degree of relationship between the two sets of scores is assessed. A statistic called the *Pearson product moment correlation coefficient*, usually abbreviated r, is used for this purpose. This statistic may range in value from -1.00 to $+1.00$; the larger the absolute value of r, the stronger the relationship. An r of 1.00 (either plus or minus) indicates a perfect relationship. An r of 0.00 indicates no relationship. The sign of the correlation coefficient indicates the direction of the relationship. When the sign is positive, then the variables are *directly related*; as scores on one measure increase or decrease, the scores on the other tend to move in the same direction. When the sign is negative, the variables are *inversely related*; scores on one measure increase as scores on the other decrease.

Finally, the correlational study, like the experiment, usually requires an inference. When the investigator computes the correlation between two measures for some sample of individuals, this alone does not permit him to generalize the relationship and assume that it would hold for other people as well. To make such a determination, tests of statistical significance are employed in correlational studies just as they are employed in experiments (*see* pp. 38–39).

As with any type of research, there are problems accompanying the correlational method. The most serious one concerns establishing causality; usually we cannot infer, when A and B are related, whether A causes B, or B causes A. For example, the question of primary interest for our purpose is, "Is viewing television violence related to violent or aggressive behavior?" The investigator collects data from many youngsters, on the amount of viewing of violent TV and the amount of aggression they engage in at school and then determines the degree of correlation. But in most instances – and without further special computation – it cannot be said that violence viewing *causes* violent behavior. For example, an equally plausible hypothesis is that children who are already aggressive *choose* to watch violence on TV. Following a summary of the major research findings of correlational studies, we shall address this problem in more detail.

CORRELATIONAL FIELD STUDIES

Early Efforts

In the mid-1950s, Himmelweit, Oppenheim, and Vince, a team of British investigators, performed the first major field study of the effects of television[4]. They studied mainly 10–14-year-old public school children, although substudies also involved younger children.

The Himmelweit project involved two major investigations. The first was a comparison of *viewers* (who had television sets in their homes) with *nonviewers* (who did not). The second investigation employed what is termed a *before-after design*. At that time, television was not available in all areas of England. The research team was therefore able to test almost all the 10–14-year-old children in a particular community, Norwich, *before* the opening of a new television transmitter, when very few families owned sets. They then retested (the *after* part of the study) 185 children who had subsequently obtained televisions and 185 who had not.

The research focused on many behaviors in addition to those relating to aggression (such as amount of time devoted to television and other activities). Diaries, detailed questionnaires, and interviews with parents were employed. Regarding aggression, teachers were requested to check whether or not each child was aggressive. The authors reported that they found no difference in aggression between the viewers and nonviewers on this measure. They did suggest, however, that differences in a variety of attitudes existed between the two groups and that[4]:

> One would expect that in the crime and detective series the constant display of aggression by both the criminal and the upholder of the law would also make an impact on those children sensitized to such cues. (p. 18)

Shortly thereafter, Schramm, Lyle, and Parker performed a series of similar studies in North America[5]. Once again, the major focus was mass media use in general, possible displacement of other activities (including time spent on homework) and television's effects on knowledge and vocabulary. However, two studies focused on aggression. The first involved children from two towns in Canada which were similar in population, types of industries, and schools but differed in one major respect: one had television, the other was so remote that television reception was impossible. The second study employed children in several towns in the Rocky Mountain area of the United States. No attempts were made to form viewer–nonviewer groups; instead the youngsters were divided into four groups on the basis of their use of television and other media: High TV–high print, high TV–low print, low TV–high print, low TV–low print. In both studies, the measure of aggression was the extent to which children indicated their agreement or disagreement with 24 statements (e.g., "I don't see anything especially wrong about a fight between two groups of teenagers; it's their business, and adults should stay out of it").

In Canada, it was found that sixth-grade boys and girls who did *not* have television were more aggressive than children who did; no differences appeared for the tenth-grade sample.

In contrast, among tenth-grade children in the United States, those in the high TV–low print group were significantly higher in aggression than those in the low TV–high print group. Results with the sixth-grade United States samples yielded no significant results, although tendencies were in the same direction. Schramm and his associates summarized their findings as follows:

> The violence on television may stimulate the aggression in an already frustrated and aggressive child. Therefore, in some, though not all, of these cases, television may both suggest the tool of violence and help build up the aggression drive that needs such a tool. Then, when aggression in a real-life situation is at a sufficient height, the child remembers how aggressive acts were done on television. (p. 161)

As in the Himmelweit work, one limitation of the Schramm study, for our purpose, is the measure of aggression; of the 24 statements rated by children only four are relevant to attitudes toward antisocial aggression. Perhaps more important, both of these investigations simply related aggression to the availability of television — *not* what the children actually watched or reported watching. The relationship of interest, of course, is between exposure to television violence (not television *per se*) and aggression.

These limitations are largely circumvented in a battery of correlational studies recently conducted for the United States National Institute of Mental Health.

The NIMH Studies

Between 1969 and 1971, under the auspices of the United States National Institute of Mental Health, approximately one million dollars was invested in a series of studies focusing on television's impact upon children. Although distributed among many research teams, the largest single block of money—about $300,000—was invested in field studies which might potentially confirm or disconfirm the relationship between television violence and aggressive behavior which had been disclosed by laboratory experimentation. Rarely before had there been such concentrated effort to answer a social scientific question.

McIntyre and Teevan's Work

Jennie McIntyre and James Teevan examined the relationship between viewing habits and deviant behavior in 2300 junior and senior high school boys and girls in a county in Maryland[6]. About 300 of the youngsters were black and the overall sample represented a wide range of socio-economic backgrounds.

To obtain information McIntyre and Teevan asked each youngster to list his four favorite programs, "the ones you watch every time they are on the air." A violence rating was assigned to each program and then an average violence score was computed for every subject. These scores were then correlated with a measure of deviance—a self-report checklist of various antisocial behaviors.

Taking a comprehensive approach, McIntyre and Teevan employed five major scales of deviance. The first measured *aggression or violent acts*, such as serious fights at school, hurting someone badly enough that he needed a bandage, and participating in gang fights. The other scales were *petty delinquency* (including trespassing and vandalism), *defiance of parents*, *political activism*, and *involvement with legal officials* (representing the more serious forms of delinquency). Answers on all five scales were scored for frequency, (0—not at all, 1—did it once, 2—twice or more). Impressively, the relationship between the various types of deviance and objective violence ratings of the four favorite programs were all positive and significant (the more violent the programs were, the greater the deviance).

McIntyre and Teevan considered not only the influence of television on deviant behavior *per se*, but also on attitudes toward deviance, especially aggression. Consistently, those whose favorite programs were violent were significantly more likely to approve of both adult and teenage violence. They concluded that[6]:

> ...*certainly television can be no more than one among many factors in influencing behavior and attitudes. However, there is consistently a significant relationship between the violence rating of four favorite programs and the five measures of deviance, three of approval of violence and one of beliefs about crime in the society. Furthermore, these relationships remain when variables expected to decrease the likelihood of deviance are introduced. The regularity with which these relationships appear suggests that they should not be overlooked.* (p. 430)

The Robinson and Bachman Study

In another major correlational study, Robinson and Bachman questioned more than 1500 older adolescents concerning their television viewing habits[7]. The subjects were asked how many hours of television they watched in an average day and what their four favorite programs were. For those who were able to list favorites, a violence viewing index was computed based on the total amount of rated violence for their favorites. This sample was divided into four groups ranging from none to high preference for violence. The measure of aggression was a self-report checklist that included eight items about serious physical aggression.

When a total score was computed, based on all eight items, (*see* Table 5.1) subjects in the three groups who reported at least some preference for violent programs were significantly more aggressive than subjects who did not list violent programs among their favorites. The same pattern was found for individual items; for example, in response to an item about getting into a serious fight at school, 50% more subjects in the high violence viewing group than in the low violence viewing group responded "yes." The tendency for those who preferred violent television to be more aggressive themselves held for most of the eight items; of particular interest is that there was a steady increase in aggression across the four groups.

Table 5.1   Percentage engaging in various aggressive behaviors according to amount of television violence viewed.

Amount of violence in four favorite programs				
	Almost none	Some	Much	Great deal
Item:	Percent	Percent	Percent	Percent
1. Gotten into a serious fight at school or work	25	30	33	37
5. Gotten something by telling a person something bad would happen to him if he didn't	15	19	20	18
9. Hurt someone bad enough to need bandages or a doctor	17	23	21	28
12. Hit an instructor or supervisor	6	7	7	11
14. Hit your father	5	8	8	8
17. Taken part in a fight where a bunch of your friends are against another bunch	19	23	24	28
18. Hit your mother	3	3	4	4
21. Used a knife or gun or some other thing (like a club) to get something from a person	2	4	3	8

Source: Robinson and Bachman[7].

Certain other variables, such as mother's education, race and previous level of reported aggression also were related to present levels of aggression, but in all subgroups those who reported a preference for (and presumably watched) a high level of violence were always the most aggressive. Robinson and Bachman concluded that television violence probably served a reinforcing or a facilitating function for subjects who were already high in aggression.

The Dominick and Greenberg Studies

Joseph Dominick and Bradley Greenberg, in another government-sponsored study, determined the amount of exposure to television violence for each of 434 fourth-, fifth-, and sixth-grade boys enrolled in Michigan public schools during the spring of 1970[8]. Exposure to violence was then related to each youngster's approval of violence and willingness to use it himself. Measures were also obtained of the degree to which the boys both perceived violence as effective and suggested it as a solution to conflict situations. As in many other studies, a familiar result was observed: higher exposure to television violence in entertainment was associated with greater approval of violence and greater willingness to use it in real life. In the investigators own words:

> *For relatively average children from average environments . . . continued exposure to violence is positively related to acceptance of aggression as a mode of behavior. When the home environment also tends to ignore the child's development of aggressive attitudes, this relationship is even more substantial and perhaps more critical.* (pp. 332–333)

Nor are such findings limited to boys. Dominick and Greenberg repeated their research, but with public school age girls. They found a pattern which closely followed that seen for the boys, reporting that for girls exposure to TV violence makes a "consistent independent contribution to the child's notions about violence. The greater the level of exposure to television violence, the more the child was willing to use violence, to suggest it as a solution to conflict, and to perceive it as effective" (p. 329).

The McLeod, Atkin, and Chaffee Reports

McLeod, Atkin, and Chaffee questioned 473 adolescents in Maryland and 151 in Wisconsin about aggressive behavior, television viewing, social characteristics of their families, and reactions to television violence[9]. The subjects were mostly white and middle class, although about 15% of the Maryland sample was black.

Violence viewing was indexed by giving each subject a list of 65 prime time programs, which had been rated for violent content, and requesting information on frequency of viewing. For each subject, the frequency score of each of the 65 programs was multipled by its violence rating. These scores were then summed to give a measure of overall violence viewing.

Self-report measures of aggression included an overall aggression score, based on (1) a 17 item scale in which the respondent was asked to judge how much each statement applied to him (e.g., "When I lose my temper at someone, once in a while I actually hit them"), (2) a behavioral delinquency scale, in which the subject was asked how often he had been in fights in school, gang fights, or achieved revenge by physical aggression, (3) a self-report scale of generalized aggression, and (4) a four item test in which the subject was presented with hypothetical conflict situations and asked to choose his most likely response among several alternatives (e.g., "Suppose someone played a real dirty trick on you, what would you do? Hit them, yell at them, ignore them, or laugh at them"). In addition to the overall aggression score, subjects were also asked about how well they control their tempers and about approval of aggression.

Reactions to television violence were assessed, including perceived learning of aggression (e.g., "Some programs give me ideas on how to get away with something without getting caught"), linkage of television violence to real life (e.g., "Action and adventure shows tell about life the way it really is"), and involvement in violent programming (e.g., "I sometimes forget that characters in these shows are just actors"). Additionally, identification with violent characters (each subject picked the TV star he would most like to resemble and the violence of that person's typical role was then rated), and their perceived efficacy were measured (e.g., "The guy who gets rough gets his way"). Finally, family environment data were gathered. The various indices included perceptions of parental control over television, parental emphasis on nonaggression, parental interpretation of television violence, parental punishment and affection, and social class. Again the results from this extensive study showed that violence viewing was significantly and positively related to self-reported aggressive behavior.

For the 151 adolescents in their Wisconsin sample, McLeod, Atkin, and Chaffee also reported data gathered from questioning others about the subjects[10]. They queried mothers on a number of items (including a comparison of the mother's own child's fighting to amount of fighting by other children, how often the child did mean things or was aggressive when he was younger, how the child would handle an argument). They asked peers for ratings on irritability, physical aggression, and verbal aggression and, for the sixth-graders, obtained teacher ratings on a four point overall aggression scale. The mothers also estimated viewing habits for themselves and for their children, and each filled out the questionnaire on family environment.

As with the self-reports, correlations between others' reports of aggression and violence viewing were significant. Additionally, the correlations between past violence viewing and present aggressive behavior were very similar to those for present violence viewing; past violence viewing was actually somewhat more strongly related to aggression than present viewing. This latter finding suggests that aggressive habits are indeed built over time by exposure to aggressive TV content.

Several family variables were related to violence viewing, including attempts to control and interpret it by parents, types of punishment used in the home, family communication patterns, and low socioeconomic status. These same variables, except for socioeconomic status, were also associated with high levels of aggression. The latter findings (and similar data collected by other investigators) confront us with the possibility that violence viewing and aggression may be related because of some additional factor—a so-called "third variable."

The Problem of Interpreting the Third Variable

The problem is that any one of these so-called third variables may lead to change in both violence viewing and aggressive behavior. Thus, viewing and aggression might vary together, producing a high correlation, although neither is causing the other. For example, parents who emphasize nonaggression may cause their children to be relatively non-aggressive and also to watch relatively little violent television. Contrarily, parents who emphasize aggression may cause their children to be aggressive and watch a lot of violent television.

It is possible, however, to assess the influence of a third variable with a procedure called the partial correlational technique. Conceptually, we want to "subtract out" the third variable's influence and see what is "left over." If the relationship (previously strong in either direction) is now reduced to insignificance, then the third variable remains a very likely candidate as a plausible cause for the relationship. If, however, the relationship that remains after "partialing" is as strong or nearly as strong as it was before, then the third variable is a poor rival hypothesis for explaining the relationship.

McLeod, Atkin, and Chaffee used partialing to analyze their findings. For their first set of data (self-reported aggression and viewing violence) they found that subtracting out the influence of total viewing time, socioeconomic status, and school performance, left the relationship unchanged. Similarly, when the effects of various types of parental punishment practices, parental affection, and perceived learning of aggression were removed, the relationship between violence viewing and adolescent aggressiveness continued to be positive and significant[9].

For the second set of data (others' reported aggression and viewing violence) partialing out the effects of total television viewing time, socioeconomic status, and school performance, again left the relationship essentially unchanged. Partialing other variables, such as parental punishment practices, parental affection, and perceived learning of aggression, reduced the correlation somewhat, but still showed that aggression based *on both others' and self-reports was associated with violence viewing*[10]. As McLeod, Atkin, and Chaffee note[9]:

> *Our research shows that among both boys and girls at two grade levels [junior high and senior high], the more the child watches violent television fare, the more aggressive he is likely to be as measured by a variety of self-report measures . . . . Partialing out [total] viewing time slightly reduces the positive correlations of violence viewing and aggressive behavior in most cases, but the basic result is the same as for the raw correlations . . . . Similarly, the partialing out of socioeconomic status and school performance does not alter the basic pattern of raw correlations . . . .* We may conclude, then, that adolescents viewing high levels of violent content on television tend to have high levels of aggressive behavior, regardless of television viewing time, socioeconomic status, or school performance. (pp. 187–191, emphasis added)

ANSWERING QUESTIONS ABOUT TELEVISION: PROCESS ANALYSIS

The partial correlational technique attempts to solve one of the problems correlational research is subject to, that of the possible influence of third variables. An additional problem remains—directionality. If we know that A and B are directly related, we still do not know whether A causes B or vice versa. Procedures can be employed in an attempt to solve the directionality problem. One, systematic process analysis, involves examining data on the various theoretical rationales which underlie each of the competing causal hypotheses.

Chaffee and McLeod have performed such a process analysis on the data presented above[11]. The two rival causal hypotheses are (H_1) that viewing television violence increases aggressive behavior, and (H_2) that aggressiveness increases television violence viewing. Each of these hypotheses assumes that some process is acting to produce the observed relationship; in other words there are secondary hypotheses, underlying each of the primary ones. Chaffee and McLeod have suggested the process analysis presented in Table 5.2.

The "learning hypothesis" (H_{1a})—derived from laboratory studies—is considered to be the process underlying H_1. Support for H_1 can be provided by demonstrating that subjects do indeed learn from television violence and realize the potential use of what they learned. McLeod,

Table 5.2   Two hypotheses about violence viewing and adolescent aggressiveness, showing secondary hypotheses involved in a process analysis.

H_1: Viewing television violence increases the likelihood of an adolescent behaving aggressively.

  H_{1a}: By viewing television violence, an adolescent learns aggressive forms of behavior; this increases the probability that he will behave in this fashion in subsequent social interaction.

H_2: Aggressiveness causes adolescents to watch violent television programs.

  H_{2a}: Aggressiveness leads to a preference for violent programs, which in turn causes the aggressive adolescent to watch them.

Source: Adapted from Chaffee and McLeod[11].

Atkin, and Chaffee measured perceived learning of aggression using the following three items[9,10]:

1. These programs show me how to get back at people who make me angry.
2. Sometimes I copy the things I see people do on these shows.
3. Some programs give me ideas on how to get away with something without being caught.

The process underlying H_2 (aggressiveness increases television violence viewing) is presumed to involve a preference for televised violence that exists previous to observing it. Thus, support for H_2 can be provided by showing that subjects who are high on measures of aggressive behavior are more likely than other youngsters to show preference for aggressive television programs. The relevant measure, then, is choice of favorite programs.

Chaffee and McLeod compared the two hypotheses as shown in Fig. 5.1. The arrows indicate the time order suggested by the two hypotheses. As can be seen from the figure, viewing violence is related to learning, and learning is related to aggressive behavior. But, although preference is related to viewing* — it is *not* related to aggressive behavior. These data, then, offer relatively clear support for the hypothesis that viewing violence causes aggression, rather than the reverse.

*Interestingly, this relationship is perhaps not as strong as might be expected. Evidently, children's violence viewing is only relatively selective and intentional; many may watch violence even though they do not prefer it (e.g., "it may just happen to be on").

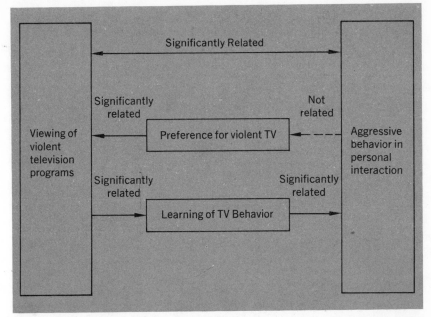

Fig. 5.1 Correlations of violence viewing, aggressiveness, and two intervening processes. Entries indicate hypothesized time order. The overall relationship is clearly accounted for more adequately by the learning path (H_{1a}) than by the preference path (H_{2a}). (Source: Chaffee and McLeod[11].)

Long-term Effects: Lefkowitz, Eron, Walder, and Huesmann

But what about long-term effects? To answer, Lefkowitz, Eron, Walder, and Huesmann used the so-called *cross-lagged panel technique* to assess the relationship between television violence viewing and aggressive behavior[12]. Earlier, Eron had determined the amount of violence viewing and aggression of 875 third-grade youngsters. Aggression was measured by peer ratings — each child rated every other child in his class on a variety of physical and verbal aggressive behaviors. A child's aggression score was determined by the number of peers who said he was aggressive. A measure of television violence viewing was obtained from an interview with each child's mother. Eron found that the boys who watched a great many violent programs were more likely to be rated high in aggressive behavior by their peers. This relationship did not hold for girls[13].

Ten years later, when the original participants were 19, Lefkowitz and his associates again obtained information about violence viewing and aggression for 460 of the original 875 subjects. The measure of aggres-

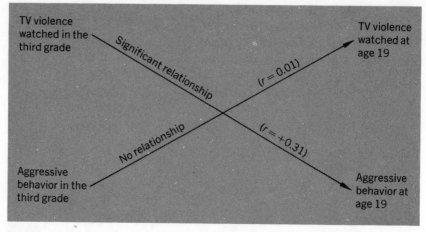

Fig. 5.2 The correlations between television violence and aggression for 211 boys over a 10-year lag (Source: Lefkowitz, Eron, Walder, and Huesmann[12]).

sion was again peer ratings based on most recent contact, with the items essentially the same as those used in the third-grade study. The data for boys are presented in Fig. 5.2 (the data collected from the girls did not reveal significant differences).

The relationship between television violence viewing in the third grade and aggression 10 years later is both positive and significant, while the one between aggression in the third grade and violence viewing when the boys were 19 is not. The pattern supports the hypothesis that viewing television violence is a long-term cause of aggressive behavior.*

---

*To understand the logic behind this conclusion more fully, consider the possibility raised in our earlier discussion of correlational studies, that a relationship will appear between overt aggression and preferences for aggressive television simply because persons who are more willing to use aggression themselves are also more likely to enjoy seeing it used by others in television dramas. This is an important "rival hypothesis" to the notion that seeing aggressive television *causes* aggressive behavior. However, if the rival hypothesis was correct, preferences for aggressive television at age 19 in the Lefkowitz study should "go together" with overt aggression in the third grade as closely as preferences for aggressive programs in the third grade go with aggression at age 19. In other words, the relationships, if accounted for by a constant third variable, should go both ways in time. In contrast, if television aggression does cause aggressive behavior later, it would be plausible to find a link between earlier television watching and later aggression but not vice versa. This is exactly what was disclosed by the Lefkowitz data.

EXPERIMENTAL FIELD STUDIES

Laboratory experiments and correlational field studies have gone far toward answering the central question, "What are the effects of televised aggression on children?" Staunch doubters, though, might still ask to see the entire process operating directly in the natural environment without the usual laboratory restrictions.

The *experimental field study* combines the naturalistic approach of the correlational study with the advantage of experimental control, and can thus provide uniquely important evidence regarding a causal relationship between televised violence and aggression by children and youth in our society.

The Steuer, Applefield, and Smith Demonstration

Steuer, Applefield, and Smith investigated the effects of aggressive and neutral television programs on naturally occurring aggressive behavior[14]. Their study involved 10 normal youngsters, enrolled in a preschool. The children, boys and girls, comprised a racially and socioeconomically mixed group who knew each other before the study began. First, they were matched into pairs on the basis of the amount of time that they spent watching television at home. Next, to establish the degree to which aggressive behavior occurred among these youngsters before any modification of their television diets, each was carefully observed in play with other children for 10 sessions, and the frequency of aggressive responses recorded. (This part of the study is referred to as the *baseline* observation phase.)

Steuer and her associates used a demanding measure of physical interpersonal aggression, including: (a) hitting or pushing another child, (b) kicking another child, (c) assaultive contact with another child which included squeezing, choking, or holding down, and (d) throwing an object at another child from a distance of at least 1 foot. The baseline established a remarkable degree of consistency within each pair, prior to the modification of televison diet.

Next, Steuer investigated the effects of television. One child in each pair observed, on 11 different days, a single aggressive program taken directly from Saturday morning program offerings, while the other member of the pair observed a nonaggressive television program. Subsequent observations of the children at play provided continuous measures of interpersonal physical aggressive behavior by each child. Changes from the original measures, if any, would have to be caused by TV effects.

By the end of the 11 sessions, the two groups had departed significantly from one another in terms of the frequency of interpersonal aggression. In fact, for every pair, the child who observed aggressive television programming had become more aggressive than his mate who watched neutral fare. As can be seen from Fig. 5.3, in most of the cases these changes were truly striking.

The Stein and Friedrich Nursery School Study

Steuer and her associates used a relatively small sample, and restricted their study to the effects of aggressive and neutral television on aggressive behavior. They controlled for, but did not investigate, the effects of other factors, such as socioeconomic status, intelligence, and amounts of home viewing. Stein and Friedrich, in one of the major NIMH studies, examined the influence of prosocial, as well as aggressive and neutral, television on several kinds of behavior; in addition, they considered several other variables that could have interacted with their experimental manipulations[15].

Subjects in the Stein study were 97 preschool children, ranging in age from 3 years 10 months to 5 years 6 months. They were enrolled in a special summer nursery school program, established for the study. The range of social class background was relatively wide, since special efforts were made to recruit children from poorer homes. The children were divided into four classes of about 25 children each, and met for $2\frac{1}{2}$ hours in either the morning or the afternoon, three times a week.

The experiment took 9 weeks to complete: 3 weeks of baseline observation, 4 weeks of controlled television viewing (the period of experimental manipulation), and 2 weeks of postviewing observation. During the period of television viewing, children were randomly assigned to one of three groups, according to type of programs seen: aggressive, neutral, and prosocial. Aggressive programs consisted of 6 *Batman* and 6 *Superman* cartoons, each containing several episodes of verbal and physical aggression. Prosocial programs were 12 episodes of *Misterogers' Neighborhood*, which emphasized cooperation, sharing, delay of gratification, persistence at tasks, control of aggression, and similar prosocial themes. Neutral programs were children's films of diverse content, which emphasized neither aggression nor prosocial behavior (almost no aggression occurred in these films, but some prosocial behavior was present). Each program lasted between 20 and 30 minutes; children in all groups saw one program a day, three days a week.

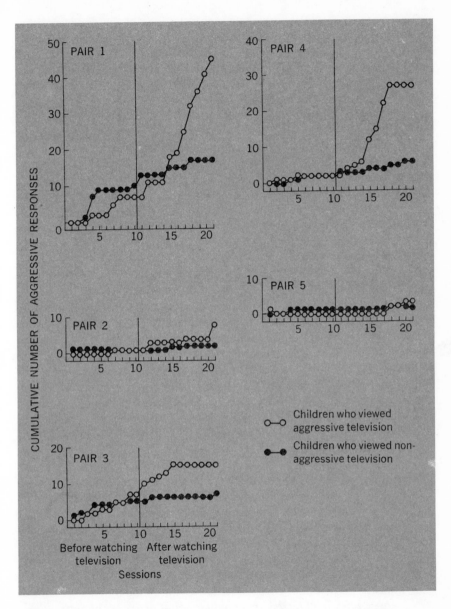

Fig. 5.3 Cumulative number of aggressive responses for children who saw aggressive and nonaggressive television in Steuer, Applefield, and Smith's experiment (Source: Steuer, Applefield, and Smith[14]).

The most important measure was observations of the children either during free-play or in the classroom. Each child was observed for 5 minutes three times each day and his behavior recorded. Behaviors were scored in five general categories: aggression, prosocial interpersonal behavior, persistence, self-control, and regression. Each category was further divided into more specific behaviors; for example, self-control included rule obedience and delay of gratification, regression included crying or pouting, and withdrawal. Observers were blind to experimental conditions; that is, they did not know to which treatment the child they were observing had been exposed.

In addition to direct observation, Stein administered a verbal-picture test of responses to frustration during the final, postviewing period of the experiment. Each child was shown cartoon pictures depicting 18 frustrating situations. He was then asked what the frustrated person would do, and was given a choice of three responses, one aggressive, one prosocial, and one avoidance.

The investigators also collected data which might relate to the child's response to the experimental treatment. Each youngster was given the short form of the Stanford Binet intelligence test. Mothers were interviewed and asked about the amount and type of television their children viewed at home. During the experimental period, each child was observed while watching television, and his attentiveness to the programs rated.

Before analyzing their data, Stein and her associates further categorized their subjects by dividing them at the median (mid-point) on the basis of their scores on three variables: IQ, socioeconomic status, and initial (preexperimental) level of aggressive behavior. (Subjects in experimental conditions were about equal in amount of aggression displayed during the preexperimental period.)

The results of this study showed that children who viewed aggressive programming were more likely to be aggressive in interpersonal situations than children who viewed neutral or prosocial television. The effect had only one limitation; it held only for those children who were in the upper half of the sample — above the median — in initial level of aggression. As the investigators point out:

> These effects occurred in naturalistic behavior that was removed both in time and in environmental setting from the viewing experience. They occurred with a small amount of exposure, particularly in relation to the amount the children received at home, and they endured during the postviewing period. (p. 247)

There is, then, a remarkable degree of convergence among all of the types of evidence that have been sought to relate violence viewing and aggressive behavior in the young: laboratory studies, correlational field studies, and naturalistic experiments all show that exposure to television can, and often does, make viewers significantly more aggressive as assessed by a great variety of indices, measures, and meanings of aggression.

But, as we noted in discussing the early Schramm and Himmelweit reports[4,5], it is not television *per se* but only some of its present offerings that appear to have this effect. In the next chapter we will see that other types of television fare can have a positive influence on the young.

REFERENCES

1. Hartley, R. L. *The impact of viewing "aggression": Studies and problems of extrapolation.* New York: Columbia Broadcasting System Office of Social Research, 1964.
2. Klapper, J. *The effects of mass communication.* New York: Free Press, 1960.
3. Singer, J. L. The influence of violence portrayed in television or motion pictures upon overt aggressive behavior. In J. L. Singer (ed.). *The control of aggression and violence.* New York: Academic Press, 1971.
4. Himmelweit, H., Oppenheim, A. N., & Vince, P. *Television and the child: An empirical study of the effects of television on the young.* London: Oxford University Press, 1958.
5. Schramm, W., Lyle, J., & Parker, E. *Television in the lives of our children.* Stanford, California: Stanford University Press, 1961.
6. McIntyre, J. J. & Teevan, J. J., Jr. Television violence and deviant behavior. In G. A. Comstock and E. A. Rubinstein (eds.). *Television and social behavior. Vol. III: Television and adolescent aggressiveness.* Washington, D.C.: U.S. Government Printing Office, 1972, pp. 383–435.
7. Robinson, J. P. & Bachman, J. G. Television viewing habits and aggression. In G. A. Comstock and E. A. Rubinstein (eds.). *Television and social behavior. Vol. III: Television and adolescent aggressiveness.* Washington, D.C.: U.S. Government Printing Office, 1972, pp. 372–382.
8. Dominick, J. R. & Greenberg, B. S. Attitudes toward violence: The interaction of television exposure, family attitudes, and social class. In G. A. Comstock and E. A. Rubinstein (eds.). *Television and social behavior. Vol. III: Television and adolescent aggressiveness.* Washington, D.C.: U.S. Government Printing Office, 1972, pp. 314–335.
9. McLeod, J. M., Atkin, C. K., & Chaffee, S. H. Adolescents, parents, and television use: Adolescent self-report measures from Maryland and Wisconsin samples. In G. A. Comstock and E. A. Rubinstein (eds.). *Television and social behavior. Vol. III: Television and adolescent aggressiveness.* Washington, D.C.: U.S. Government Printing Office, 1972, pp. 173–238.
10. McLeod, J. M., Atkin, C. K., & Chaffee, S. H. Adolescents, parents and television use: Self-report and other-report measures from the Wisconsin sample. In G. A. Comstock and E. A. Rubinstein (eds.). *Television and social behavior. Vol. III: Television and*

adolescent aggressiveness. Washington, D.C.: U.S. Government Printing Office, 1972, pp. 239–313.

11. Chaffee, S. H. & McLeod, J. M. Adolescents, parents, and television violence. Paper presented at symposium. "The Early Window: The Role of Television in Childhood," American Psychological Association Convention, Washington, D.C., September 1971.

12. Lefkowitz, M. M., Eron, L. D., Walder, L. O., & Huesmann, L. R. Television violence and child aggression: A followup study. In G. A. Comstock and E. A. Rubinstein (eds.). *Televison and social behavior. Vol. III: Television and adolescent aggressiveness.* Washington, D.C.: U.S. Government Printing Office, 1972, pp. 35–135.

13. Eron, L. D. Relationship of TV viewing habits and aggressive behavior in children. *Journal of Abnormal and Social Psychology,* 1963, **67**, 193–196.

14. Steuer, F. B., Applefield, J. M., & Smith, R. Televised aggression and the interpersonal aggression of preschool children. *Journal of Experimental Child Psychology,* 1971, **11**, 442–447. (© Academic Press, Inc.)

15. Stein, A. H. & Friedrich, L. K. Television content and young children's behavior. In J. P. Murray, E. A. Rubinstein, and G. A. Comstock (eds.). *Television and social behavior. Vol. II: Television and social learning.* Washington, D.C.: U.S. Government Printing Office, 1972, pp. 202–317.

6

TELEVISION'S POTENTIAL: PROSOCIAL EFFECTS

A critic has argued that television is an electronic Pied Piper[1], leading our children into a sea of undesirable and harmful influences. Certainly, in view of the effects of televised violence on children's aggressive behavior and their approval of violence, this analogy does not appear terribly farfetched. But need it be this way? Is it necessarily true that television does not—or at least potentially cannot—lead its viewers to more favorable outcomes?

Most investigations into the medium's influence focus on deviant behaviors, perhaps because of the dramatic quality of fistfights and shootouts, recent fears of increasing crime rates, and concern over national involvement in unpopular wars. Yet there are examples of cooperative effort, of helping, and of sharing on many of today's programs. Even essentially violent programming offers instances of prosocial action; the detective may be extremely altruistic toward his office help and the gun-toting criminal cowboy may help the widow retain her land.

We know relatively little about the effects of these examples, as they appear in their present context. But we do know, from recent studies both in the laboratory and in the field, that television has a vast potential for inculcating positive lessons. In this chapter we will examine some of the evidence for television's potential—as it relates to prosocial actions, efforts to remedy behaviors that are usually judged debilitating and more formal educational programming designed to teach specific content.

STUDIES OF PROSOCIAL BEHAVIORS

Teaching Sharing Through Television

The value placed by society on sharing is clearly shown in the adage that it is more blessed to give than to receive. But sharing is not innately built into the human organism—as any parent of a 2-year-old can testify. It must be taught in the manner in which society attempts to teach all its values, by providing direct instruction and appropriate examples.

Bryan and Walbek[2] investigated the effects of both these teaching techniques—through simulated television programs—on children's sharing. In one study, third- and fourth-grade youngsters were taken individually to a research trailer and permitted to play a bowling game for ten trials. When they scored high, they received a gift certificate which could be exchanged for money or prizes. The children were informed that they could donate their winnings to the March of Dimes if they wished. After each child played the game for a while, he saw a TV program of another child of the same sex playing the game. The other child, a model, was either generous, donating one-third of his winnings, or selfish. For two groups, the model also made statements about sharing, preaching either greed or generosity, while in the third no such statements were made. After viewing the program, each child played the game again and was given the opportunity to share in private. This test of prosocial behavior revealed that children who saw a charitable television model were significantly more likely to share than those who saw a greedy one, regardless of the nature of the preachings.

This finding does not apply only to third- and fourth-grade subjects. In his laboratory, Bryan has tested over 550 children ranging in grade from one to five and coming from diverse geographic areas[3]. It is further supported by many studies that show a similar positive influence with live altruistic or selfish models[4,5].

Increasing Self-control

Using essentially the same procedure, Stein and Bryan demonstrated that a televised model also can induce self-control[6]. Third- and fourth-grade girls viewed a sequence which showed a peer model playing the bowling game; half of the subjects saw a skilled model who won often, while the other half saw an unskilled model who won less frequently. In either case, the model was instructed to reward herself, according to a stringent rule, by taking a stack of nickels each time she obtained a certain high score.

The children were subdivided into four groups according to the model's preaching and practicing of the rule. Either she preached and practiced rule adherence, preached and practiced rule breaking, or was inconsistent in what she said and what she did. Then each child played the game herself. The measure of rule adherence was the number of nickels the child took on nonwinning trials. Those who viewed a model who both preached and practiced rule adherence followed the stringent self-reward rule more than those who saw a model who preached and practiced transgression. Children who viewed an inconsistent model broke the rule the most.

Another form of self-control—resistance to temptation—can also be influenced by television examples. As the name suggests, an individual is put into a situation in which he can transgress (cheat on tests, steal, and so on) in order to gain a reward. The person has the option of resisting or not resisting the "temptation" he is faced with. Walters, Leat, and Mezei brought 5-year-old boys into a room equipped with many attractive toys and a dictionary[7]. Each boy was firmly instructed not to play with the toys, although he could look at the dictionary. In their subsequent treatment, the lads were divided into three groups. The control group did not see a film. The model-rewarded group saw a film in which a little boy played with the forbidden toys; his mother entered and joined in these activities. In a model-punished condition, youngsters saw a film in which a boy played with the toys but was scolded when his mother entered.

Each youngster was then left alone, while hidden observers measured how much time he spent playing with the toys and how long it took before he played with them. Those who saw the film with the punished model waited much longer before deviating and spent less total time playing with the toys than boys in either of the other groups. In fact, most of those in the model-punished group did not play with the forbidden toys at all, while children in the model-rewarded group played with the forbidden toys longer and sooner than anyone else.

Wolf further investigated the effects of televised models on resistance to deviation[8]. He exposed 5-, 7-, and 9-year-old boys to a peer model, presented on television, who said he was going to follow the rule not to play with certain toys, or said he would break the rule. Boys who saw the deviant model played with the forbidden toys more than those exposed to a conforming model or no model. Boys who saw the obedient exemplar played with the toys less than subjects who saw no model. Thus the television model increased behavior like his own, regardless of what he did.

We can see from laboratory studies that a variety of positive acts can be facilitated by the observation of televised models. These investigations interestingly are "true-to-life"; they create situations that each of us actually encounters – viewing someone being rewarded or punished for a behavior, or observing an individual whose action and preaching do not always coincide. Nevertheless, they still can be criticized on the grounds that they are laboratory studies (*cf.* pp. 68–69).

The presence of one prosocial program on national television, *Misterogers' Neighborhood*, has allowed a recent field study of television's effects to overcome these criticisms. Fred Rogers began developing his program in the 1960s for the Canadian Broadcasting Company. In the United States, the show began on NET in 1967; it is now carried by over 200 stations. A typical program begins with Mister Rogers arriving "home" and changing into leisure attire. As he does so he sings "Won't You Be My Neighbor" and begins talking directly to his audience about things of interest to children, e.g., possible crises such as moving or the death of a pet. Additionally, he frequently reassures children about common fears such as of being bitten by animals. Puppets are also used to deal with similar problems. He continually emphasizes to his youthful watchers that "There's only one person in the whole world like you, and I like you just the way you are."

The work of Stein and Friedrich, mentioned in Chapter 5, examined the effects of such presentations. Recall that these researchers observed children in classroom and play situations[9]. Each child was observed for 9 weeks, 3 weeks prior to treatment, 4 weeks during the treatment, and 2 weeks afterward. Every schoolday the children saw either *Misterogers' Neighborhood*, aggressive cartoons, or neutral programs. In addition to recording aggressive behaviors, the observers also recorded three categories of prosocial behavior: persistence (e.g., independence and refusing help), interpersonal prosocial behavior (e.g., cooperation, mature social skills), and self-control (e.g., rule obedience).

Socioeconomic status and IQ, previously assessed by the investigators, influenced what prosocial lessons were learned. Self-control was influenced in the predicted ways: children in the prosocial condition increased while those in the aggressive condition *decreased*. On the prosocial interpersonal measure, only the children in low socioeconomic classes responded as might be expected, increasing in prosocial behavior.

An additional analysis of responses to frustration suggested that:

> *Children in the Aggressive and Neutral conditions manifested patterns of frustration and aggression that would be expected, but children in the Prosocial condition did not show increased aggres-*

sion with increased frustration to the same extent. Instead, children in the Prosocial condition manifested increased prosocial behavior in conjunction with increased frustration; children in the Aggressive condition showed reduced prosocial behavior with increased frustration. (p. 263)

POTENTIAL THERAPEUTIC EFFECTS OF TELEVISION

Another positive potential use of television is the development of courage in children[10]. It is well known—by parents and teachers as well as by professional counselors—that children may fear an extensive range of events and situations. Frequently these fears seem to create only small discomfort, and "spontaneously" disappear. In other cases, though, they may cause considerable discomfort to the child and his family and be quite persistent. Live modeling of fearlessness is one way in which children can be helped to overcome them. Evidence also exists that film and television programs can markedly reduce fear.

Bandura and Menlove, for example, showed children who were very fearful of dogs (as measured by willingness to approach and play with a cocker spaniel) a series of such programs[11]. In the experimental conditions, fearful children saw other children playing with dogs. In the control condition, they were shown movies of Disneyland and Marineland. After seeing the experimental displays, the previously frightened children were much more willing to play with dogs than the children in the control group. (*See* Fig. 6.1.) Indeed, comparison of Fig. 6.1 and Fig. 4.1 (p. 155) shows dramatically how an imitative process may govern both antisocial and prosocial behavior in the same way.

In a similar study, 18 preschool boys who would not approach a German shepherd either saw no film or viewed one designed to reduce fear[12]. In the treatment film, a fearless lad played with a dog while a younger, obviously fearful boy watched. Gradually the second boy imitated the fearless behavior; as the film ended both youngsters were playing with the animal. On a posttest, 8 of the 9 boys who viewed the film were willing to approach the German shepherd. In contrast, those who had not seen it remained afraid.

From the same laboratory—and using essentially the same imitation procedure—has come some evidence for reduction of fear of the dentist through a simulated television program[13]. In the film, while an 8-year-old boy climbs fearlessly into the dental chair and has a dental examination and cleaning, a fearful 4-year-old girl looks on. As the story progresses,

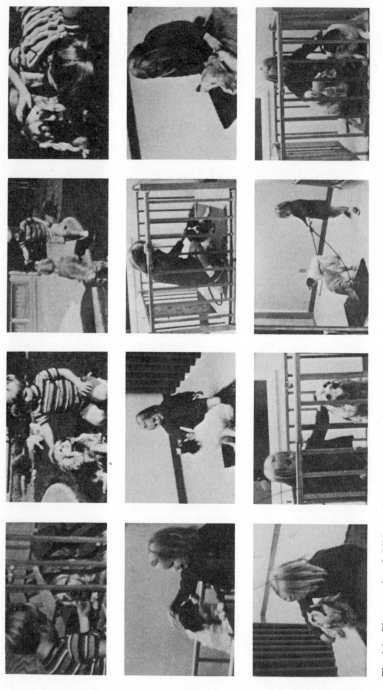

Fig. 6.1 Photographs of children who were apprehensive about dogs engaging in fearless interactions with them after exposure to the series of specially designed films (Source: Courtesy of Dr. Bandura).

the little girl's fear subsides and when her turn comes, she too climbs unafraid into the dental chair and is treated. The program was viewed by $4\frac{1}{2}$–$6\frac{3}{4}$-year-olds who were reported by their parents as being afraid of the dentist. The youngsters were then shown pictures of a dentist, fireman, farmer, physician, and policeman and were asked whom they would like to visit at their place of work. Those who had viewed the film were more willing to visit the dentist than fearful children who had seen no film.

Thus, we are beginning to accumulate evidence that witnessing fearlessness in a television-like format can indeed help children overcome fearful situations through the process of imitation. With its mass audience, television obviously has potential for explaining how to deal with fearful events and demonstrating that certain situations, such as those involving dental care, are not as terrible as might be expected. Let us look at one more related example of this potential for bringing about behaviors most of us would judge beneficial.

From children who had just entered preschool, Robert O'Connor selected 12 who had been isolated from other youngsters and who showed striking withdrawal behaviors[14]. Some of these children viewed a neutral film about dolphins, while the remainder saw a film depicting appropriate nursery school behavior; both were shown on a television. The treatment film was divided into 11 scenes, each showing an activity that was more threatening than the one preceding it in terms of vigor of play and size of the group involved. In each scene an initially withdrawn peer model observed an activity, then joined in, receiving some form of positive encouragement from other children or the narrator. For example, in the first scene the model came to share a book with a neighbor; in the last one, he joined 6 other children who were gleefully throwing a toy about the nursery school.

For his test, O'Connor observed his subjects in the nursery school setting. Children who had seen the film about dolphins were as withdrawn as they had been at the beginning of the study. But those who had viewed the social-interaction program significantly and dramatically increased the number and quality of interactions with their peers. Figure 6.2 shows the average number of social interactions for each group, before and after the viewing period.

O'Connor's conclusion emphasized the potential power of television:

It should be noted . . . that the experiment achieved significant changes in social behavior among children with relatively severe deficits without developing a therapeutic relationship. Until recent-

ly, a fairly intimate client-therapist relationship and the attainment of insight have been considered necessary conditions of personality change. In contrast [these results obtained] using only a television-like format indicate that the social behavior of children can be effectively enhanced [by such efforts]. (p. 246)

The O'Connor study is not only dramatic in its effects but, like the Stein and Friedrich investigation, was carried out in a naturalistic setting. As we shall see in the next section, examination of the influence of educational televison also has this desirable feature.

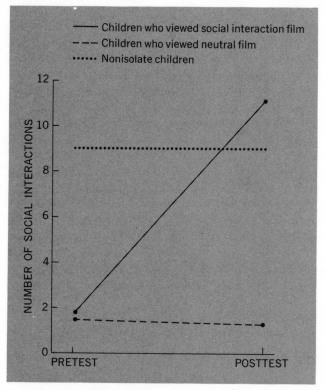

Fig. 6.2   Number of social interactions displayed by withdrawn children before and after viewing either a social interaction or neutral TV film. The dotted line represents social interaction shown by 26 nonisolate children who were observed at the pretest phase of the study (Source: O'Connor[14]).

EDUCATIONAL TELEVISION

One of the interesting facts emerging from surveys of a large number of people is that many think television, any television, is educational. Parents most often mention education as its major advantage for children, and most sixth- and tenth-grade subjects in one study said that they learn during at least some of the time they spend viewing[15,16]. Adults are convinced that they themselves learn as well[17,18].

> *Respondents say they derive lessons and solutions to real-life problems from soap operas and acquire medical knowledge from "doctor" programs. Several respondents also mentioned learning about methods of tracking and catching criminals from police-detective series ...* (p. 588)[18]

These reports concern what might be considered incidental learning, in that the programming referred to was designed essentially for entertainment. There is little doubt that people do, indeed, learn incidentally from such shows. Further, there is increasing effort to use television as a tool for the teaching of specific content.

The Development of Educational Television

In the United States, educational television exists both on a national and a local level. The latter involves the use of closed-circuit systems. For example, the South Carolina Educational Television Center transmits lessons to over 250 schools presenting a complete kindergarten through college curriculum. Thirty-seven schools in Hagerstown, Maryland have used a complete television curriculum since 1956[19].

The only countrywide educational television system is a loosely federated organization of about 100 stations—the National Educational Television Network (NET). Initial attempts to designate channels exclusively for educational programming were bitterly fought by commercial networks who argued that all of television was their domain. But, in 1952 the FCC set aside a number of UHF channels for educational purposes.

By 1959 there were 45 actual educational stations—some community operated, some university owned, and some operated by school systems. On the average, they were on the air 5 days per week, almost 9 hours a day. An analysis of the content of their offerings revealed the following: (1) credit course use—40%, (2) children's (out of school) viewing—13%, and (3) adult (noncourse credit) viewing—47%[20]. Differences in program

Table 6.1 Comparison of programs offered by commercial and educational television in 1959.

Type of program	Commercial TV	Educational TV
News	7%	3%
Sports	6%	1%
Children's	7%	8%
Music	4%	9%
Other Entertainment	62%	1%
Information	14%	78%

Source: National Educational Television and Radio Center[20].

content between educational television and commercial fare are illustrated in Table 6.1.

In 1959, only 8.5 million homes were capable of receiving a noncommercial station; many were not close enough to a transmitter and others could not receive UHF. Still, assuming multiple viewers in each home, educational television then had a *potential* audience of about 25 million. But a survey by the American Research Bureau revealed that only about 2 million people watched at least one program during a typical week. This small group was found to differ from "the average TV viewer" on several dimensions. They tended to be better educated, to come from higher social strata, to spend less total time viewing, and to be more planful and selective in their viewing habits[21].

The first decade of educational television saw the whole enterprise on a financial precipice. But in 1962 federal legislation authorized the expenditure of funds for the construction and equipment of stations. Significant growth then began, and by 1965 NET was functioning much as it does today.

Children's Programs on Educational Television

The goal of children's commercial television is to sell products; its content is primarily violent with little eye toward the possible effects of continued exposure to murder and mayhem. But two alternatives have appeared recently on educational television—*Sesame Street* and *The Electric Company*—which are remarkably different. They are essentially nonviolent and educationally oriented, and yet retain entertainment values. Both were begun only after extensive planning, and ongoing research has been set up to examine their effects and ensure that their goals would be met.

Sesame Street

Educators have increasingly recognized the importance of preschool experiences for later educational development. But four-fifths of our 3- and 4-year-olds and one-quarter of our 5-year-olds do not attend school. In an attempt to fill this void a group of public and private agencies (The Carnegie Corporation, Ford Foundation, U.S. Office of Education, U.S. Office of Economic Opportunity, and the National Institute of Child Health and Human Development) established the Children's Television Workshop. Its goal was to telecast a daily program that would both entertain and foster intellectual and cultural development[22].

In 1968 a series of planning seminars was held by experts in child development, preschool education, and television production. Out of these meetings came ideas for many of the basic instructional methods and ways of presenting materials. The planning phase went even further. Viewing preferences of youngsters were examined and the attention-holding power of videotaped materials was assessed by playing them in competition with potential distractors. Already, a striking contrast is evident with the usual way in which commercial programs are developed for children (*see* Chapter 2).

In 1969, *Sesame Street* was on the air, combining attention holding tactics (e.g., fast movement, humor, slapstick, and animation) with a carefully planned educational curriculum designed to foster skills such as recognition of the letters of the alphabet, recognition of the numbers 1 through 10, simple counting ability, vocabulary, and the like (*see* Fig. 6.3). Because of the specificity with which goals were stated, evaluation of the educational effectiveness of the program was not only possible but included in the overall plans.

The Electric Company

In 1970, another team from the Children's Television Workshop began planning a program aimed specifically at reading skills. As with *Sesame Street*, *The Electric Company* grew out of a series of consultations with experts—this time in the area of reading. Prior to the first appearance of one of the shows, various reading curricula had been evaluated and experimental programs pretested[23].

In the fall of 1971 the series began with a snappy format. Well-known personalities such as Bill Cosby frequent the show and heavy use is made of animation. The curriculum, directed primarily at second-graders, involves what is termed sound-symbol analysis of the printed word.

Fig. 6.3 *Sesame Street*, Muppets Ernie (*left*) and the Cookie Monster give a lesson on the letter *D* and words that begin with *D* in this segment from the educational television series for preschoolers. The Muppets, created by Jim Henson, make regular appearances on the show to help teach such skills as the alphabet and counting. *Sesame Street*, now seen on more than 250 stations across the country, is a production of Children's Television Workshop (Source: Courtesy of Children's Television Workshop).

Children are taught the correspondence between letters (and combinations of letters) and sounds to enable them to decode words. Reading for meaning, using the context of the material, and syntax are also taught. A cartoon sequence illustrating how a child learns to properly locate an adverb is presented in Fig. 6.4.

Does Sesame Street Teach?

Although evaluation for *The Electric Company* is not yet available, Samuel Ball and Gerry Bogatz of The Educational Testing Service (which runs college boards among its many other testing activities) have completed an independent assessment of *Sesame Street*[22].

The first year's studies were conducted in five widely separated areas of the country. Children were assigned either to a control condition or to a viewing condition, involving home or nursery school viewing. In the case of home viewers, parents were told about *Sesame Street*, given publicity material about the program, and were visited each week by members of the research team. The control subjects did not receive these treatments. In the school situation the experimental classrooms received two television sets, while control classes did not. According to Ball and Bogatz:

> *It was generally understood that the teachers of the viewing classes would use the sets to have their pupils view* Sesame Street *but that the degree to which they did so, and the way* Sesame Street *was used in the classroom, was their prerogative.* (p. 19)

In both school and home samples, the experimental treatment lasted about 6 months. Altogether, about 950 children participated in all phases of the study. Although the research team made efforts to control the amount of watching in both home and school viewing groups, the lack of full control over viewing constitutes a problem in the study.

Each child was both pretested and posttested. The tests were designed to measure the specific learning goals; thus, there were subtests on Body Parts, Letters, Numbers, Forms, Matching, Relationships, Sorting, and Classification. An example is shown in Fig. 6.5.

Parents also were interviewed, both before and after the study, about their attitude toward education, the child's viewing habits, and the "intellectual climate" in the home (e.g., how many books does the family own?).

Ball and Bogatz analyzed their data in several ways. Besides examining

Fig. 6.4 Learning to position adverbs. *The Electric Company* method (Source: Courtesy of Children's Television Workshop).

Here are pictures of shoes. Which picture doesn't belong with the others?
Which is different from the others?

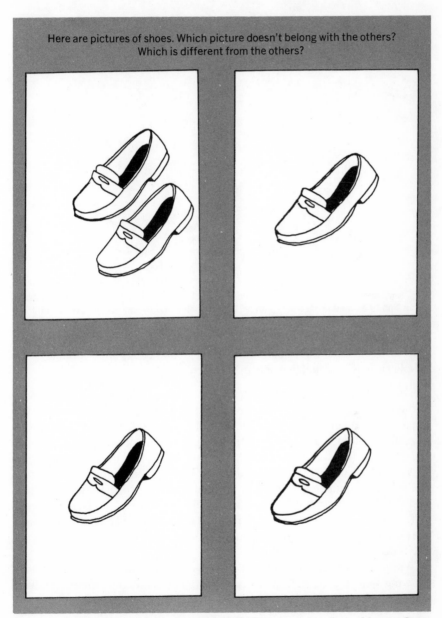

Fig. 6.5 Sample item from the tests given to children to assess the effects of *Sesame Street* (Source: Ball and Bogatz[22], courtesy of Children's Television Workshop).

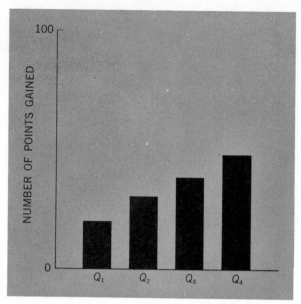

Fig. 6.6 Improvement in total test scores for children grouped into different quartiles according to amount of viewing (Source: Based on Ball and Bogatz[22], courtesy of Children's Television Workshop).

a total score and then separate subtest scores, they also looked at the whole sample and then subsets of children.

Total sample. The original plan to compare viewers to nonviewers turned out not to be feasible because most of the subjects watched at least occasionally.* Instead, the sample was divided into quartiles (a quartile contains 25% of the sample) on the basis of amount of viewing. Q_1 rarely watched *Sesame Street*; Q_2 watched two or three times a week, Q_3 about four or five times a week, and Q_4 more than five times. Because the different quartiles differed in original level of proficiency on the pretest, the investigators decided to assess change scores, that is, the average differences between pretests and posttests. As Fig. 6.6 indicates, the more that children watched the program, the more they tended to improve on the total score.

When the total score was broken down, it was clear that the effects of viewing held for all eight major subtests. The gains on some items were

*This problem, while somewhat ironic as the initial concern was over whether *anybody* would watch, testifies to the popularity of the program.

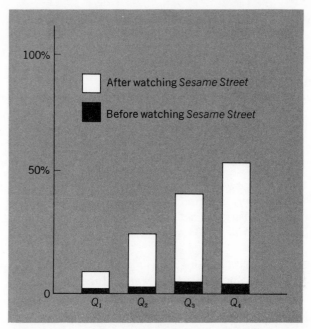

Fig. 6.7   Percentage of children who recited the alphabet correctly, grouped according to quartiles of amount of viewing (Source: Based on Ball and Bogatz[22], courtesy of Children's Television Workshop).

quite impressive; alphabet recitation, for example, on which the various groups were about equal at the beginning, had improved dramatically among children who watched *Sesame Street* regularly. (*See* Fig. 6.7.)

Disadvantaged children. When middle-class and Spanish speaking children were taken out of the sample, 731 disadvantaged youngsters remained. Unfortunately, these children tended to watch the program less often, and so were disproportionately highly clustered in the lower viewing quartiles. However, those who watched did improve on total test scores. Statistical analysis indicated that the effects held for several subgroups: "... viewers gained more than nonviewers, at home as well as at school. Boy viewers benefited similarly to girl viewers." (p. 312)

These gains were significantly greater for viewers on all the subtests, except for body parts, where a ceiling effect was apparently operating.*

---

*Many children already had this knowledge so there was a limit (ceiling) on the treatment's ability to show an effect.

Children who viewed at home seemed to improve more than those who viewed at school, probably because they had somewhat lower scores to begin with. Still there was significant improvement in both cases (one implication is that, as hoped, professional teachers are not necessary for benefiting from *Sesame Street*).

Of particular interest, in considering the gains in specific subtests, are scores on items and skills not directly taught on *Sesame Street*. For example, *Sesame Street* apparently had some effect on reading skill, and ability to write one's first name, both of which are important for school performance. (*See* Fig. 6.8.)

> *For the disadvantaged group the six items in the reading subscale were significantly affected by amount of viewing despite the fact that reading words was* not *a* Sesame Street *goal nor was it directly taught on the show.* (p. 319, original emphasis)

Advantaged children. Sesame Street was also effective in teaching middle-class children, most of whom watched the program five or more

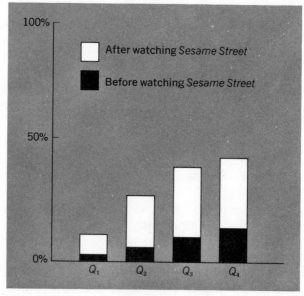

Fig. 6.8   Percentage of children who wrote their first names correctly, grouped according to quartiles of amount of viewing (Source: Ball and Bogatz[22], courtesy of Children's Television Workshop).

times a week. The gains, while significant, were not as sharply differentiated across the viewing quartiles. One possible explanation, once again,
is a ceiling effect; many of these children learned all they could from the
program in a small amount of viewing, and had essentially achieved the
goals set by the *Sesame Street* staff. Of particular interest is a comparison
of advantaged and disadvantaged children. Not surprisingly, the advantaged children were substantially better at pretest. After viewing *Sesame
Street* for one season:

> *Although advantaged children who viewed retained their compara-
> tively high attainments vis-à-vis disadvantaged children, the
> margin of difference was lowered. Disadvantaged children who
> viewed a lot surpassed the advantaged children who did not view
> or who viewed very little . . . . At pretest, all disadvantaged quartiles
> were below the comparable advantaged quartiles in terms of test
> scores. At posttest there was considerable overlap among advan-
> taged and disadvantaged children.* (p. 209)

Spanish speaking children. A pilot study with 43 Chicano youngsters
was conducted in Phoenix, Arizona. The authors appropriately cautioned
against overgeneralizing from the results, but the findings are of some
interest. All children tended to score lower on the pretest than the rest of
the sample, and most fell into the lowest viewing quartile. Nevertheless,
gain scores among those who did view the program five or more times per
week were quite large, in fact, larger than for the rest of the sample.

Recent Innovations

A later investigation provided some additional information[24]. By this
time, *Sesame Street* itself had changed somewhat; for example, practice
in sight-reading a 20-word vocabulary of common words, and simple
skills in Spanish had been introduced. Evaluation changed to incorporate
these expanded goals, but the major focus of the tests was the same. Two
other types of measures were also added: questions designed to examine
attitudes toward race, school, and other people, and teacher rankings of
school readiness, at the beginning and end of the school year.

A new sample of children was selected, in cities where *Sesame Street*
had not been available the first year. This sample was restricted to urban
disadvantaged children. The investigators also followed up 283 of the
disadvantaged children studied during the first year. About half of these
children had started in nursery school, kindergarten, or first grade.

The results essentially replicated those of the first year study—children who viewed *Sesame Street* improved more than children who did not. The follow-up study also revealed that heavy viewers were rated by teachers as better prepared for school than low viewers, and adapted well to the school situation. The children who viewed frequently continued to outgain low viewers, particularly on the items introduced during the second year of the program. The show influenced other behaviors as well: viewers scored significantly higher on measures of attitudes toward school and toward people of other races.

An additional analysis indicates that *Sesame Street* has positive effects on vocabulary. Also, a reanalysis of first year total test scores compared the effects of the program on disadvantaged black and white children. As can be seen in Fig. 6.9 the two groups do not differ from each other; both can benefit from regularly watching *Sesame Street*. A similar analysis, comparing advantaged and disadvantaged children, indicates that *Sesame Street* can help to close the gap between these two groups.

We have seen that television has a great—though largely unrealized—potential for educating and teaching positive lessons to our young. What keeps it from doing so? One answer lies in the fact that interest in the prosocial influence of television is a recent phenomenon based on data

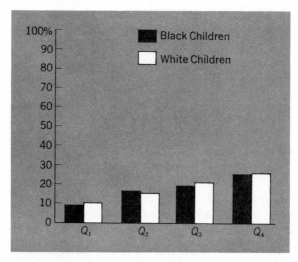

Fig. 6.9 Comparative gains on total test for black and white disadvantaged children, grouped according to quartiles of amount of viewing (Source: Bogatz and Ball[24], courtesy of Children's Television Workshop).

gathered only in the last few years. But another answer lies in the commercial structure of television and its influence on program content. In the next chapter, then, we will examine the commercial interests, how products and programs are sold, and how the content of American children's television has become a continuous chain of often questionable, sometimes dangerous advertisements.

REFERENCES

1. Witty, P. A. Some research on TV. In S. Sunderlin (ed.). *Children and TV: Television's impact on the child.* Washington, D.C.: Association for Childhood Educational International, 1967.
2. Bryan, J. H. & Walbek, N. B. Preaching and practicing generosity: Children's actions and reactions. *Child Development*, 1970, **41**, 329–353.
3. Bryan, J. H. Children's reactions to helpers: Their money isn't where their mouths are. In J. Macauley and L. Berkowitz (eds.). *Altruism and helping behavior.* New York: Academic Press, 1970.
4. Bryan, J. H. & London, P. Altruism behavior by children. *Psychological Bulletin*, 1970, **73**, 200–211.
5. Krebs, D. L. Altruism—an examination of the concept and a review of the literature. *Psychological Bulletin*, 1970, **73**, 258–302.
6. Stein, G. M. & Bryan, J. H. The effect of a television model upon rule adoption behavior of children. *Child Development*, 1972, **43**, 268–273.
7. Walters, R. H., Leat, M., & Mezei, L. Inhibition and disinhibition of responses through empathic learning. *Canadian Journal of Psychology*, 1963, **17**, 235–243.
8. Wolf, T. M. A developmental investigation of televised modeled verbalizations of resistance to deviation. *Developmental Psychology*, 1972, **6**, 537.
9. Stein, A. H. & Friedrich, L. K. Television content and young children's behavior. In J. P. Murray, E. A. Rubinstein, and G. A. Comstock (eds.). *Television and social behavior. Vol. II: Television and social learning.* Washington, D.C.: U.S. Government Printing Office, 1972, pp. 202–317.
10. Bryan, J. & Schwartz, T. Effects of film material upon children's behavior. *Psychological Bulletin*, 1971, **75**, 50–59.
11. Bandura, A. & Menlove, F. L. Factors determining vicarious extinction of avoidance behavior through symbolic modeling. *Journal of Personality and Social Psychology*, 1968, **5**, 16–22.
12. Hill, J. H., Liebert, R. M., & Mott, D. E. W. Vicarious extinction of avoidance behavior through films: An initial test. *Psychological Reports*, 1968, **22**, 192.
13. Poulos, R. W. & Davidson, E. S. Effects of a short modeling film on fearful children's attitudes toward the dental situation. Unpublished manuscript. State University of New York at Stony Brook, New York, 1971.
14. O'Connor, R. D. Modification of social withdrawal through symbolic modeling. In K. D. O'Leary and S. G. O'Leary (eds.). *Classroom management.* New York: Pergamon Press Inc., 1972.
15. Steiner, G. *The people look at television.* New York: Alfred A. Knopf, 1963.
16. Lyle, J. & Hoffman, H. R. Children's use of television and other media. In E. A.

Rubinstein, G. A. Comstock, and J. P. Murray (eds.). *Television and social behavior. Vol. IV: Television in day-to-day life: Patterns of use.* Washington, D.C.: U.S. Government Printing Office, 1972, pp. 129–256.

17. LoSciuto, L. A. A national inventory of television viewing behavior. In E. A. Rubinstein, G. A. Comstock, and J. P. Murray (eds.). *Television and social behavior. Vol. IV: Television in day-to-day life: Patterns of use.* Washington, D.C.: U.S. Government Printing Office, 1972, pp. 33–86.

18. Robinson, J. P. Toward defining the functions of television. In E. A. Rubinstein, G. A. Comstock, and J. P. Murray (eds.). *Television and social behavior. Vol. IV: Television in day-to-day life: Patterns of use.* Washington, D.C.: U.S. Government Printing Office, 1972, pp. 568–603.

19. Dizard, W. P. *Television: A world view.* Syracuse: Syracuse University Press, 1966.

20. National Educational Television and Radio Center, The content of educational television. In W. Schramm (ed.). *The impact of educational television.* Urbana, Illinois: University of Illinois Press, 1960.

21. Schramm, W. The audiences of educational television. In W. Schramm (ed.). *The impact of educational television.* Urbana, Illinois: University of Illinois Press, 1960.

22. Ball, S. & Bogatz, G. A. *The first year of Sesame Street: An evaluation.* Princeton, N.J.: Educational Testing Service, 1970.

23. Fowles, B. Building a curriculum for "The Electric Company." In *The Electric Company: An introduction to the new television program designed to help teach reading to children.* New York: Children's Television Workshop, 1971.

24. Bogatz, G. A. & Ball, S. *The second year of Sesame Street: A continuing evaluation.* Princeton, N.J.: Educational Testing Service, 1972.

7

THE COMMERCIAL INTERESTS

In the early days of broadcasting, when radio was just beginning to have a major impact, it was assumed that programming would be financed by radio set manufacturers, not by advertisers. Indeed, in 1922 Herbert Hoover remarked, "It is inconceivable that we should allow so great a possibility for service, for news, for entertainment, for education . . . to be drowned in advertising chatter."

But advertising did come to radio, although with a promise that the intrusion would be minimal. For example, "In 1929 the National Association of Broadcasters published a code insisting that 'commercial announcements, as the term is generally understood, shall not be broadcast between seven and eleven P.M.'"[1]. That this promise went unfulfilled is all too common knowledge. The most frequent complaint about television today concerns commercials, referring to both their timing (amount of time, number of interruptions) and content[2]. Nonetheless, the commercial lies at the heart of network television.

THE STRUCTURE OF COMMERCIAL TELEVISION

Selling Time

Commercial television is designed to make money for the networks. It has succeeded admirably well; in 1970 the networks and stations enjoyed net revenues of almost 3 billion dollars through advertising[1]. The transaction underlying this success, in the oldest traditions of barter, involves selling time — "minutes" in the industry jargon* — to advertising agencies or directly to potential sponsors. The networks, by tradition, offer 6 minutes per hour during prime time and 12 during daytime programming; in addition, the stations themselves sell time in the periods surrounding the programs.

When the networks sell, they do not simply offer a spot to a prospective buyer. Rather, a package of time is sold, with minutes on shows of varying quality and attractiveness and at a package price which is negotiated according to time, network and, of course, the acumen of bargainers. But the prices are not wholly arbitrary, even if they fluctuate. The Nielsen ratings are used to determine the number of homes which a particular show ostensibly visits. Then advertisers compute their cost for reaching each thousand homes. By this logic a show which reaches 10 million families with spots at $40,000 per minute and one which reaches 8 million families at $32,000 per minute are equal in cost: $4 per thousand homes. That, by the way, is a high rate; *Flip Wilson* at an estimated $4.25 per thousand, and a rate of $86,000 per minute of commercial time, appears to hold something of a record.

To illustrate the vastness — and growth — of the amount spent on TV advertising, we can consider the actual dollar expenditures of leading advertisers. In 1966, the top 15 advertisers spent over 900 million dollars. By 1969 over 1 billion dollars was spent on TV spot advertising alone and the figures have continued steadily upward since then. In a single 3-month period during 1970 almost 100 advertisers spent more than 1 million dollars *each* on TV spot commercials with some spending more than ten times that amount (*see* Table 7.1); and the business keeps growing. The April 24, 1972, issue of *Broadcasting* reported[3]:

> ... *spot [advertising] business in first quarter 1972 was up over 1971 in virtually every case. Increases ranged from a low of 3–4% to a high of 13–14%. In general, the gain came to about 10% in the first quarter.* (p. 21)

The United States has far more advertising on children's television than does any other country in the world; in fact, most other nations in the free world do not permit *any* advertising on shows directed toward the young. Even among those nations where commercial messages are per-

---

*The term "minutes" is a euphemism, though, since it usually refers to 30-second advertising spots.

Table 7.1 Estimated expenditures of the top 25 national and regional spot-television advertisers in the last 3 months of 1970.

Company	Expenditure ($)
1. Procter & Gamble Co.	13,604,700
2. General Foods Corp.	12,101,300
3. American Home Products Corp.	6,760,500
4. Colgate-Palmolive Co.	6,331,700
5. General Mills	5,988,800
6. Loews Theatres	5,700,400
7. Lever Brothers Co.	5,606,400
8. Popeil Brothers	4,863,200
9. R. J. Reynolds Industries	4,746,200
10. Sterling Drug	4,226,600
11. Coca-Cola Co.	3,858,000
12. PepsiCo Inc.	3,499,900
13. Bristol-Myers Co.	3,444,900
14. Warner-Lambert Pharma. Co.	3,322,000
15. British-American Tobacco Co.	3,183,600
16. Deluxe Topper Corp.	3,131,000
17. Ideal Toy Corp.	3,130,800
18. Ronco Tele-Products	3,116,300
19. William Wrigley Jr. Co.	3,050,600
20. Gillette Co.	2,996,300
21. Kraftco Corp.	2,910,800
22. Philip Morris	2,817,000
23. Alberto-Culver Co.	2,807,800
24. Quaker Oats Co.	2,780,200
25. C. P. C. International	2,752,700

Source: *Broadcasting*, April 19, 1971.

mitted, they appear much less often than in the United States (*see* Fig. 7.1)[4].

Hearings before a United States Senate subcommittee, released in the spring of 1972, indicate that children's programming can be, and usually is, a goldmine with our present heavy saturation of advertising[5]. In 1970, for example, advertisers spent, and the networks received, 75 million dollars for advertising time on network children's shows alone. Weekday network shows and local reruns of old cartoons swell the figure even more. Relatively few advertisers supply this money: Kellogg, Mattel, and General Mills account for 30% of total revenues and five other companies—General Foods, Deluxe Topper Toys, Quaker Oats, Miles Laboratories, and Mars—account for an additional 25%.

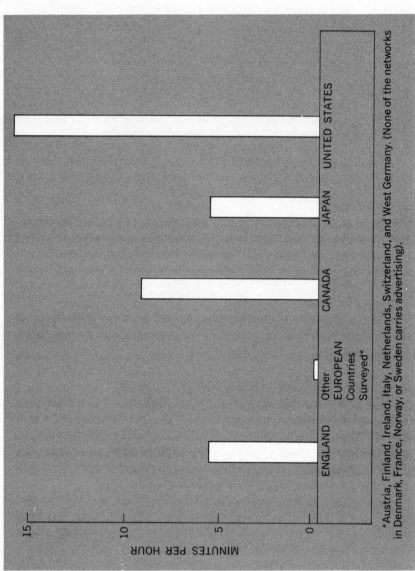

Fig. 7.1 Amount of advertising allowed on network children's television (Source: Courtesy of the National Citizens Committee for Broadcasting).

*Austria, Finland, Ireland, Italy, Netherlands, Switzerland, and West Germany. (None of the networks in Denmark, France, Norway, or Sweden carries advertising).

Balanced against the large gross revenues are very low program costs— about $10,000–$11,000 per half hour. That quality is sacrificed for revenue can be seen clearly through some specific examples: *Bugs Bunny* and *Road Runner* alone grossed more than $2\frac{1}{2}$ million dollars in 12 months; *Tom* and *Jerry* yielded $1\frac{1}{2}$ million dollars in a comparable period; the insipid but violent *Spiderman* cartoon series was good for more than $250,000 in just 3 months.

Advertisers, of course, are interested in selling their products. Thus, they want to reach the largest possible number of people with their commercial messages and are willing to pay more money for spots on programs with large audiences. The ratings, to which we turn next, are supposed to provide them with the information necessary for making decisions about where to invest their advertising dollars.

The Ratings

The value of any particular commercial minute depends upon the popularity, or presumed popularity, of the show on which it appears. Ratings thus play a vital role in the commercial enterprise of television.

The rating system came in virtually with the television set; a group of advertisers formed an organization to telephone people to ask them what they had watched the night before. The technique was a questionable one—respondents have been found to make strong evaluative comments about nonexistent shows.

So the phone call was soon supplanted by the diary, which then became the preferred mode of obtaining a family's self-report of viewing patterns. But the diaries, too, proved to be fallible. For example, the respondent is supposed to fill them out daily, but[1]:

> *One suspicious investigator distributed a hundred diaries, telling recipients he would be back to pick them up in seven days—and then returned in five days instead. He found a number of diaries still blank, the householder having put off till tomorrow what he forgot to do today—and an almost equally large number already complete for all seven days, the helpful respondent having gone through* TV Guide *at once and written in the shows the family "always" sees.* (p. 37)

Still, diaries are often used to obtain ratings at the local and regional level, and so continue to play a role in determining both the advertisers' budgets and what we—and our children—see. For commercial purposes, though, an effort has been made to overcome the problems of the diary by mechanization; we refer to the Nielsen system.

The Nielsen Ratings

Among inveterate TV viewers *Nielsen* is almost a household word. For network shows it is these evaluations that mercilessly determine which of our favorite offerings will be made to suffer an untimely death at mid-season and which will be granted near immortality by network high priests.

The Nielsen evaluations come from machines — the patented Audi-meters of the A. C. Nielsen Company. About 1200 families are paid 50¢ a week so that the company's device can record the activity of their television sets. Nielsen then sells the information for an undisclosed amount, estimated at about 10 million dollars a year[1].

Buyers believe they are getting their money's worth. But the Nielsen system — and a similar one used by Britain's commercial network, the Independent Television Authority — can only indicate whether the set is on or off and the location of the channel selector. Whether anyone is in the room — much less watching the show or commercial message — is simply ignored. Yet we know that television viewing is frequently a secondary activity; the set often "just runs" while people read, wash dishes, and eat their meals. The real question of interest to advertisers, "How much watching actually occurs?" is not adequately addressed by Nielsen.

It has now been answered, at least in part, using a technique developed by Robert Bechtel and his associates[6]. They located videotape cameras in people's homes so that as the family watched television the television watched the family. This permitted careful, complete and reliable comparisons of diary reports and simple measures of when the set was on (the Nielsen method) with what and how much was actually viewed.

The results were startling. First, both the Nielsen and the diary techniques consistently overestimate — by a factor of 30–50% — actual viewing of television. Second, the amount of viewing that occurs when the set is on varies substantially with type of program: movies, for example, are watched 76% of the time while on, sporting events less than 60%, and commercials, literally at the bottom of Bechtel's list of eleven types of program events, 54.8% of the time. (*See* Table 7.2.) Neither a diary nor a Nielsen audimeter could have told us that.

We see then that important decisions, concerning the amount of money spent for advertising minutes and which programs live or die, have been

Table 7.2 Program categories ranked by percentage of time watched while program is on.

Percentage of time watched while program was on	
Program type	%
Movies	76.0
Children's	71.4
Suspense	68.1
Religious	66.7
Family	66.4
Game show	65.9
Talk show	63.7
Melodrama	59.3
Sports events	58.7
News	55.2
Commercial	54.8

Source: Bechtel *et al.*, 1972, p. 294.[6]

based on information which is, at best, questionable. Further, the amount of attention paid to commercials is low. Perhaps this is not surprising, given the frequent complaints against advertisements.

COMPLAINTS AGAINST COMMERCIALS

Frequency

One irritated viewer watched less than half of the movie *Shake Hands with the Devil*, during which time he counted 20 commercials! The movie *Rebel Without a Cause* was interrupted six times in less than an hour, with each interruption good for two or three commercials[7]. Robert Choate, chairman of the Council on Children, Media, and Merchandising, reports that there are about 20 ads per hour during children's programming and 2–12 per hour during adult prime time hours[8].

As Newton Minow, a former FCC Commissioner, noted[9]:

Today, at professional football games, the most important man on the field does not wear shoulder pads or football cleats; nor is he dressed in the striped shirt and white duck pants of a game official. This most important man is easy to identify because he wears a bright red hat and upon his signal activity begins or stops. The man in the red hat is on the field to make certain that competitive action never interferes with the television commercial messages of the sponsors. He nearly always removes the red hat after one team has scored, and he does not put it back on his head until a television director tells him, through a portable telephone, that the commercial is completed. When the red hat returns to his head, the referee allows the game to continue. (p. 13)

Stereotypes

The frequency of television commercials is not the only basis on which they have been judged objectionable. Many people have argued that their content, too, is antagonistic to the public interest because it presents prejudicial or distorted views of the world. For example, Marya Mannes has charged television with sustaining many cultural stereotypes about women's roles[10]:

> *...television commercials...reinforce, like an insistent drill, the assumption that a woman's only valid function is that of wife, mother, and servant of men: the inevitable sequel to her earlier function as sex object and swinger. [Mannes suggests that only four types of women appear in TV ads] the gorgeous teen-age swinger with bouncing locks; the young mother teaching her baby girl the right soap for skin care; the middle-aged housewife with a voice like a power saw; and the old lady with dentures and irregularity.... Only one woman on a commercial...has a job; a comic plumber pushing Comet. (pp. 66–67)*

Similarly, the National Organization for Women (NOW) studied over 1200 commercials and reported that[11]:

> *Almost all of them showed women inside the home. In 42.6 per cent they were involved in household tasks; in 37.5 per cent they were domestic adjuncts to men, and in 16.7 per cent they were sex objects. That doesn't leave very many, and a lot of commercials don't even have people in them. Only 0.3 per cent showed women as autonomous people leading independent lives of their own. (p. 12)*

The insulting nature of women's roles can best be demonstrated by role reversal[11]:

> *Maybe the best consciousness-raiser would be to turn the ads around in a kind of reverse degradation, and show men slinking*

around in tight bikinis being ogled by appraising female eyes, or eating spoonfuls of Light 'n Lively in the reducing salon while the camera panned slowly up their legs. "Minute by minute, you become a man again," a condescending female voice-over would tell him as he soaked in the tub with his Softique. (p. 50)

Commercials aimed particularly at children also foster stereotypes, both sexual and racial[12]. One investigator, for example, monitored Saturday children's television on the commercial stations in Boston. He found that ads containing only males outnumbered ads containing only females by three to one. Further, of 13 ads showing only girls, 8 were doll commercials and a ninth was a cereal commercial offering a doll as a premium. Almost all of the ads showing only boys involved toys, including boats, planes, cars, and puzzles.

The advertisements were also biased regarding the race of the characters; they were overwhelmingly white. Eighty-three different commercials showed only white characters, but just one ad showed only blacks (featuring Willie Mays in a cereal commercial). Although 20% of the ads were "integrated," that usually meant showing a crowd of white children with a single black or oriental face among them.

Certainly television commercials are not the only aspect of American society, or even American television, which portray women and minority groups in limited or undesirable roles, or suggest that these roles are the only appropriate ones for them However, like the entertainment programs which they support (*see* Chapter 2), they are an important source of children's expectations — and prejudices.

Undersirable Influences on Program Content

The commercial aspect of television does not end with the advertisements; the sponsor's arm often extends into the programs with which he is associated, however peripherally.

Newton Minow has remarked on the tragic difference in the relationship between advertisers and content in newspapers and magazines versus television. In the former, there is a clear separation between advertiser and content; the advertiser buys space but does not influence what is written. In television, decision-making about program content has fallen into the hands of the advertising agency[9].

A classic tragic example of this lopsided emphasis occurred during a showing, sponsored by the natural-gas industry, on the

> *program "Playhouse 90" of a drama dealing with the Nuremberg war trials, under the title, "Judgment at Nuremberg." Viewers noticed that a speech by actor Claude Rains about the killing through cyanide gas of thousands of concentration-camp prisoners by Adolf Hitler's Third Reich was abruptly interrupted by a deletion of words. The editing was done by a CBS television network engineer while the videotape recording of the drama was on the air. The words eliminated were "gas chamber." This editing, called "blipping," was done to accommodate the sponsor. A broadcasting executive later explained: "...we felt that a lot of people could not differentiate between the kind of gas you put in the death chambers and the kind you cook with . . ." (p. 14)*

Similarly in *The Courtship of Eddie's Father*, breakfast scenes could not include the family eating bacon and eggs—since one of the sponsors was a cereal manufacturer. When Camel cigarettes sponsored *Man Against Crime* (a series running from 1949 to 1954), the show's writers were instructed[13]:

> *Do not have the heavy or any disreputable person smoking a cigarette. Do not associate the smoking of cigarettes with undesirable scenes or situations plot-wise. (p. 23)*

Arson was not one of the crimes committed on this show—that might remind viewers of fires started with cigarettes. Nor, for that matter, was anyone supposed to cough on *Man against Crime*; that, too, might be suggestive of the ills of smoking[13].

The heavy hand of the ad man may also have contributed to the early demise of dramatic offerings on television. In the early 1950s, the "Golden Age" of television provided exciting and popular drama. Writers like Paddy Chayefsky penned some of the classic plays of television; anthologies like *Philco Television Playhouse* and *Goodyear Television Playhouse* presented complicated and disturbing problems without easy solutions. Commercials presented problems too, complete with solutions—a new shampoo or floor wax—appropriate to their triviality. The contrast was too great for the advertisers. They began to assert their power, first distorting the more provocative programs, and finally refusing to pay for them. The anthologies began to die, and they have not yet revived. One critic suggests that the industry does not want good drama[14]:

> *TV is not an art form or a culture channel; it is an advertising medium. . . . [Therefore] it seems a bit churlish and un-American*

of people who watch television to complain that their shows are lousy. They are not supposed to be any good. They are supposed to make money ... in fact, "quality" may be not merely irrelevant but a distraction. (p. 7ff.)

One former network news executive, Fred Friendly, charges that the advertisers have come to control more than entertainment. They exert a subtle influence on news as well—not by directly censoring it, but by limiting the time devoted to it. News "minutes" do not sell. Friendly commented[15]:

Three soap companies—Procter & Gamble ... Colgate-Palmolive ... and Lever Brothers—account for about 15 percent of the nation's total television sales. This is one reason why Americans know more about detergents and bleaches than they do about Vietnam or Watts. The three great [networks] ... are so oriented to advertising and merchandise that after a single day of viewing television, a visitor from another planet could only infer that we are bent on producing a generation of semiliterate consumers. (pp. 294–295)

Friendly conducted a running battle with CBS executives for years over the need to inform the public. When CBS chose to air *I Love Lucy* reruns rather than Senate hearings on the Vietnam War, Friendly decided he had lost the battle, and resigned.

ADVERTISING DIRECTED AT CHILDREN

"And a little child shall lead them—to your product."

The area of advertising which has drawn the most fire is commercials aimed at children. Robert Choate reports that half of all children's advertising sells food, another 30% toys, and 10% vitamins[8]. Almost all the food ads are for sweetened products and snack food—candy, cookies, soft drinks, sweetened cereals, and the like. Meanwhile, the opportunity to advertise wholesome foods which naturally contain needed vitamins has long been overlooked. As one group concerned with children's television observes[16]:

Yet a child watching television programs for children sees ads for sugared cereals, candy, snack foods and sugared drinks in an unceasing barrage and learns nothing of the essentials for a balanced diet. On a typical Saturday morning a child will see no ads for fruit, vegetables, cheese, eggs or other valuable nutritional foods but instead will be cajoled to buy a new sugared cereal with a toy premium or to put syrup into his milk to make it "fun". (pp. 2–3)

Choate charges that "television today has produced an accelerated deterioration in eating practices in the world's most wealthy nation. Nutrition is human ecology and television is a master polluter." (p. 147) Yet, these ads bring a large financial reward[1]:

The exploitation of children's appetites ... brought the networks nearly a quarter of their total profits for the year [1970–71]. (p. 161)

ACT

Perhaps the most outspoken, and certainly the most successful, critic of TV commercials for children has been *A*ction for *C*hildren's *T*elevision. The organization began in 1968 when Mrs. Peggy Charren of Boston called a meeting of mothers in her home to discuss the high frequency of violence on children's television programs. Another founder of the organization, Mrs. Judith Chalfen explained the viewpoint which emerged[17]:

We found it was a curious kind of violence .... It never seemed to produce any lasting harm to people. That's an odd concept to be giving children, isn't it—that violence doesn't hurt anybody? But our main objection is that the programs don't do anything for the kids. The cartoons are just mindless chase sequences. For instance, nobody has ever tried to explain the moon shots to 7-to-11-year-old children on television. (p. 21)

ACT has taken the stance that deficient programming can be traced to the advertisers and sponsors and that the road to improvement is through pressure on them. Its work has now come to focus most heavily on the commercials themselves, to reduce their frequency and, perhaps more important, to eliminate misleading or potentially dangerous content. One area of concern has been with ads for vitamins and other edibles.

Vitamin Ads

ACT is particularly concerned about the advertising of vitamins as being "just like candy." The pills are still medicine, not candy. Yet, as

Table 7.3   Chocolate Zestabs Commercial.

On Saturday, November 27, 1971, at 8 : 18 a.m. on the CBS Television Network, station WHDH-TV, channel 5, in Boston, the following one minute commercial for Chocolate Zestabs made by Sauter Laboratories was aired during "The Bugs Bunny Show," a children's television program:

Dialogue	Action
	View of Prof. Chocolate's factory from outside.
Prof. Chocolate: Hello my little sweet ones. I'm Professor Chocolate. Here's some of my famous inventions.	Prof. C., animated cartoon character talking.
Chocolate chip cookies.	Elves shoot chocolate chips from cannons at revolving assembly lines of plain cookies.
Chocolate sundaes. I invented it on Monday.	Elves making sundaes as they move along conveyor belt.
Chocolate milk. First I had to invent a chocolate cow.	Cow straddling conveyor belt carrying milk bottles and elf milking cow to fill bottles with chocolate milk.
And now my greatest invention chocolate vitamins.	Holds and points to bottle of Chocolate Zestabs.
New delicious Chocolate Zestabs. Chocolate inside, beautiful colors outside. Oh Angelo, you're an artist.	Angelo: an elf, is holding paint palette and painting the vitamin pills as they are carried along on conveyor belt.
Mom . . . kids don't always eat right. One Chocolate Zestabs gives them all the vitamins they normally need in a day along with their favorite thing to eat, chocolate.	Elves shoveling vitamins into a bottle.
Ummm, delicious.	Prof. C. eats vitamin.
New delicious Chocolate Zestabs.	Still shot of display of Chocolate Zestabs.

Source: Courtesy of Action for Children's Television.

illustrated in the advertising copy shown in Table 7.3, children are being encouraged both to dose themselves and to rely on artificial supplements to make up for poor eating habits. ACT has documented that vitamin pills are the second most common form of poisoning among children under the age of 5. Although the bottles contain the warning—in miniscule letters—"Keep out of the reach of children," the ads for them are directed seductively toward the youngsters. Vitamins will make you big and strong, they promise, as they virtually order toddlers to buy them. Occasionally, a child can be too convinced. ACT points out that 4-year-old Erin Shelton, of Overland, Kansas, took 40 Pals vitamins after seeing one such ad, so that he would "grow big and strong real fast." After having his stomach pumped he was kept in intensive care for 2 days; his mother was permitted to see him for 5 minutes every hour. Luckily, Erin recovered.

In July of 1972, ACT scored a major victory. Three major drug companies—Miles Laboratories, Bristol-Myers, and Hoffman-LaRoche—acceded to the pressure which the organization had mounted and agreed to end the advertising of vitamins on children's television. (They had spent $4 million on advertisements of vitamins on network children's television shows in 1971.)

In a letter to Peggy Charren, ACT's president, the vice-president of Miles Laboratories wrote[18]:

> *We have become increasingly convinced that continued advertising of our children's vitamin supplement products in the present type of environment of children's television programs had become no longer in our interest; this relates especially to some of the highly questionable programming as well as the number and nature of commercials presently being aired in the Saturday morning time period.*

Toy Advertising

The advertising of toys to children has become one of television's major commercial efforts. On a single Saturday morning shortly before Christmas, 1969, NBC children's programs carried 55 toy commercials—and it was at the bottom of the list! ABC had 62 such commercials and CBS had 63 on the same morning.

Heavy advertising campaigns for children began, according to a comprehensive summary prepared by ACT, in 1955[19]. That was the year that Mattel launched a TV-based advertising program that propelled it from a $500,000 concern to a truly big business of $12 million. The lesson of Mattel's example was not lost on other companies, especially when the firms which elected to advertise in this way made appreciable inroads into others' markets. Playskool, a subsidiary of the Milton Bradley Co., began television advertisements of its products in 1969. The parent company's annual report explains why[20]:

> *For years, Playskool's best advertising was the high quality and play value of its merchandise. Parents told friends about these durable, lovable toys, and children often passed them down from one to another through a growing family. In 1969, however, mounting competitive pressures indicated that if growth were to continue, Playskool must present a strong national promotional program. For the first time, the company launched a campaign on network television . . . (p. 14)*

Bringing the Store into the Living Room

The fact that toy advertisements, directed at children, appear on television would not be — and perhaps should not be — objectionable if the presentations were tasteful displays of the availability of the product. But they are not.

There is a conscious and deliberate move on the part of the ad-makers to capitalize on all of the child's weaknesses, to bring the toy store into the child's living room, as one executive put it, so that a purchase is almost inevitable. Another, in the same vein, has said[21]:

> *When you sell a woman on a product and she goes into the store and finds your brand isn't in stock, she'll probably forget about it. But when you sell a kid on your product, if he can't get it, he will throw himself on the floor, stamp his feet and cry.* You can't get a reaction like that from an adult. (emphasis added)

Yet a third executive, knowing his target and ready to move in, wrote[22]:

> *Sooner or later you must look through kid's goggles, see things as they see them,* appeal to them through their childish emotions *and meet them on their own ground.* (emphasis added)

ACT is also concerned about ads selling toys, since many break easily when they are taken home, or do not meet the claims made for them in the commercials. Research has confirmed that many such advertisements are misleading[12]. In ads displaying dolls, for example, the picture usually shows a doll almost filling the screen, with a small child in the background;

this is a very effective technique for distorting the size of the toy. (Other commercials simply show the product—without any background of common objects which would make a size judgment possible.) Another deceptive practice is the addition of qualifiers to very seductive descriptions—usually quickly at the end of the ad. Once again, the doll commercials provide a good illustration: in the last few seconds an off-stage voice says "accessories and costumes sold separately." So the parent who buys the doll in question will soon be asked by a disappointed youngster to purchase a host of unanticipated—and expensive—extras as well.

In testimony before the Federal Trade Commission in November 1971, Dr. Earle Barcus[23] noted that what was not in commercials was as important as what was. Few ads (10 out of 132 in one study) give any indication of product cost. Research shows that children's commercials rarely state what the product is made of, how it works, its price or size, what age group it is designed for, or how long it can be expected to last.

In late 1970, ACT attempted to get free time to counteract toy commercials during the Christmas period[24]. Although they failed, their efforts to regulate children's advertising have continued.

EFFECTS OF TV ADVERTISING ON CHILDREN

What are the effects of the enormous number of TV commercials aimed at children? The question has many facets: How much attention do children pay to commercials? How well do they understand them? How much credence do they put in the message? Centrally important, do the commercials lead children (who themselves have little money) to pressure their parents to buy advertised products?

Until recently, surprisingly little was known about the effects of commercials. Research conducted by the networks and advertisers is unavailable to the public but there appears to be relatively little of it. Many ads are made intuitively; they are designed to appeal to the adult sponsors and admen who buy and pay for them, and may or may not appeal to the children for whom they are made. It is often said that the commercials are the most entertaining feature of American television. Perhaps this is true for the adult connoisseur of the ridiculous but it does not characterize the reactions of the young. More precise knowledge of these reactions has become available through a series of sophisticated studies by Scott Ward and his associates, at the Harvard Graduate School of Business Administration.

Children's Attention to Commercials

In one study, mothers served as observers, recording whether the child attended to the commercials (had his eyes consistently on the screen), whether he liked the commercials, and information about the commercial itself. Each mother observed her child's behavior during at least 6 and not more than 10 one-hour periods spread over 10 days[25].

The most often watched commercials occurred during children's programs and movies, although there were age differences reflecting changing tastes in programming. The types of commercials naturally varied with the type of program, so that younger children were more likely to see commercials for food, gum, and toys and games, while older viewers were more likely to be exposed to commercials for personal products. For all

Table 7.4   Children's attention to commercials.

		Saturday morning (6 a.m.–1 p.m.) Age		Weekday evening (6 p.m.–1 a.m.) Age	
		5–8	9–12	5–8	9–12
Attention during commercial	Full	50%	33%	46%	45%
	Partial	15	20	21	24
	Up, in room	3	13	11	4
	Talks	18	16	16	18
	Up, leaves	9	9	2	3
	Not in room	6	9	4	6
		100%	100%	100%	100%

Attention stimulation by commercials: behavior during commercials among children paying full prior attention to programming, by age group

		Age group		
		5–7	8–10	11–12
Subsequent attention to commercial	Full attention	78%*	70%	57%
	All other (partial attention, talking, up in room, leaves room)	22	30	43
		100%	100%	100%

*Should be read: Of all observations of 5–7-year-old children paying full prior attention to programming, 78% of the subsequent observations indicated that these children continued to pay full attention to commercials.

Source: Adapted from Ward, Levinson, and Wackman[25].

children, the commercials at the beginning of the program held attention best, although children paid less attention to all commercials than to the program itself.

Other results, some of which are shown in Table 7.4, indicate that attention often falls off when the commercial comes on. Among the older children who were engrossed in the program which preceded the commercial, barely more than half (57%) continued to devote their full attention to television when the commercial appeared.

Reactions to Commercials

This lack of attention to commercials may be related to children's views of their purpose, validity, and credibility. Ward and his colleagues interviewed children about their interpretations of advertisements[26]. Important age differences captured in the examples below, appeared in the youngsters' reactions.

UNDERSTANDING OF INTENT

Kindergarten: confused (some thought "information," others "didn't know"), semirecognition that ads were intended to sell
Example: (Q: What are commercials for?) "If you want something, so you'll know about it. So people know how to buy things. So if somebody washes their clothes, they'll know what to use. They can watch what to use and buy it."

Second grade: clear recognition that advertisements were intended to sell; semirecognition of advertisers' motives
Example: (Q: What are ads for?) "To make you buy (product)." (Q: Why do they want you to buy it?) "So they can get more money and support the factories they have."

Fourth and Sixth Grades: clear recognition of purpose of commercials, motives of advertisers, and emerging understanding of the techniques advertisers use in constructing commercials
Example: Fourth Grade: "They put the free things inside so you'll buy it (cereal box)." (Q, referring to discussion of the staging, "tricks" etc., advertisers use: Why do they do that?) "Because they want you to buy it." Sixth Grade: "To advertise the product, to make people buy it, to benefit them because then they get more money." (p. 457)

ABILITY TO DIFFERENTIATE THE PRODUCT BEING ADVERTISED FROM THE ADVERTISING MESSAGE ITSELF

Kindergarten: no discrimination between advertisement and product advertised

Example: (Q: What's an ad that you liked?)
"I like the one about the space men." (Q: Why?) "It was Hostess Twinkies."

Second Grade: confusion (can like product but not like commercial, but confuse product advertised with advertisement?)

Example: (Q: Which commercials did you like?) "Well, I like the advertisements about model electric shavers...I don't like those about blades, that are called shavers, because they cut and I don't think its good to use those kinds of shavers."

Fourth and Sixth Grades: clear differentiation between advertisement and product advertised

Examples: Fourth Grade. "I like that ad (for coffee), its so funny I just love it!" (Q: If you had to buy coffee, would you buy that brand?) "I don't know...I don't even drink coffee."

Sixth Grade: "It (an Alka Selzer advertisement) was really funny I just love it!" (Q: If you had to buy coffee, would you "I've tried it and it made me even sicker."

In a more extensive investigation a larger sample of children responded to similar questions[27]. As can be seen in Table 7.5, clear age differences again emerged in children's understanding of the purpose of commercials.

Table 7.5   Children's understanding of the purpose of commercials, by age group.

	Degree of Understanding		
	Low (Confused, unaware of selling motive; may say "commercials are for entertainment.")	Medium (Recognition of selling motive, some awareness of profit-seeking; "commercials are to make you buy things.")	High (Clear recognition of selling and profit-seeking motives; "commercials get people to buy and they pay for the show.)
Age			
5–7	55%	35%	10%
8–10	38%	50%	12%
11–12	15%	60%	25%

Source: Ward, Reale, and Levinson[27].

Most of the youngest children's responses were in the lowest category of understanding, e.g., "commercials are to help and entertain you." In contrast, by age 11–12 most children understand the nature of the adman's mission, e.g., "commercials are to make people buy things." A similar age trend was found for the perceived credibility of commercials (*see* Fig. 7.2). Note the striking and growing cynicism which appears even before adolescence. Why do children lose faith in commercials? Ward and his associates report[27]:

> *When asked why commercials tell the truth or do not tell the truth, 24 of the 33 older children (ages 9–12) said they feel that the commercials are untrue because the motives of the commercials are suspect—e.g., "they just want to make money" ... (p. 485)*

Almost 40% of the 9–12-year-olds were already of the opinion that the products offered to them on TV are often "not like the ads say."

Effects on Purchasing

The ultimate test of commercials, of course, is in the arena of purchasing. Ward and Wackman questioned mothers about the frequency of their children's attempts to influence purchases[28]. The highest frequency

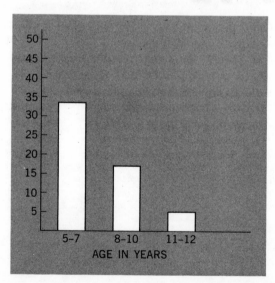

Fig. 7.2 Percentage of children who believe that commercials always tell the truth, as a function of age (Source: Based on data presented in Ward, Reale, and Levinson[27]).

of requests was for games and toys — by the youngest children. Food products, especially those relevant to children such as breakfast cereal, snack foods, candy, and soft drinks, were requested very frequently by children in every age group; otherwise, younger children were generally more likely to try to influence parental purchases than were older ones. But even though they tried harder, they were less successful than their more persuasive seniors; mothers reported yielding more often to the requests of older than of younger children.

In sum, by age 11 children have become cynical about the purpose and credibility of commercials, feeling that they are being lied to in an attempt to get them to buy products which are not as desirable as the adman's copy would have it. It is not surprising, then, that children do not pay full attention to the ads and that as they grow older they less often try to influence parental purchases.

We have examined the content of television and its effects on children, and see a clear need for change. With few exceptions, the commercial interests have failed to make a positive contribution to television; often they have played a role with distinctly negative effects. We turn now to the issue of regulating TV content, examining the roles played by the U.S. Government and the industry itself.

REFERENCES

1. Mayer, M. *About television*, New York: Harper & Row, 1972.
2. LoSciuto, L. A. A national inventory of television viewing behavior. In E. A. Rubinstein, G. A. Comstock, and J. P. Murray (eds.). *Television and social behavior. Vol. IV: Television in day-to-day life: Patterns of use.* Washington, D.C.: U.S. Government Printing Office, 1972, pp. 33–86.
3. Spot-TV getting up a head of steam. *Broadcasting,* April 24, 1972.
4. Fleiss, D. & Ambrosino, L. *An international comparison of children's television programming.* Washington, D.C.: National Citizens Committee for Broadcasting, 1971.
5. Pearce, A. The economics of network children's television programming. U.S. Congress, Senate. Hearings before the Subcommittee on Communications, March 1972.
6. Bechtel, R. B., Achelpohl, C., & Akers, R. Correlates between observed behavior and questionnaire responses on television viewing. In E. A. Rubinstein, G. A. Comstock, and J. P. Murray (eds.). *Television and social behavior. Vol. IV: Television in day-to-day life: Patterns of use.* Washington, D.C.: U.S. Government Printing Office, 1972, pp. 274–344.
7. Tobin, R. L. Spots before our eyes. *Saturday Review,* February 14, 1970.
8. Choate, R. B. The sugar-coated children's hour. *The Nation,* January 31, 1972.
9. Minow, N. N. *Equal time: The private broadcaster and the public interest.* New York: Atheneum, 1964. (Copyright© 1964 by Newton N. Minow. Reprinted by permission of Atheneum Publishers.)
10. Mannes, M. Television: The splitting image. *Saturday Review,* November 14, 1970.

11. Hennessee, J. A. & Nicholson, J. NOW says: TV commercials insult women. *The New York Times Magazine*, May 28, 1972. (Copyright © 1972 by The New York Times Company. Reprinted by permission.)

12. Barcus, F. E. Saturday children's television: A report of TV programming and advertising on Boston commercial television. *Educational Resources Information Center*, 1972, 7(2).

13. *Blueprint for Man Against Crime.* Cited in E. Barnouw, *A history of broadcasting in the United States, Vol. III—from 1953: The image empire.* New York: Oxford University Press, 1972. (Copyright© 1972 by Erik Barnouw.)

14. Karp, D. TV shows are not *supposed* to be good. *The New York Times Magazine.* January 23, 1966. (Copyright© 1966 by The New York Times Company. Reprinted by permission.)

15. Friendly, F. W. *Due to circumstances beyond our control.* New York: Random House, 1967. (Copyright © 1967 by Fred W. Friendly. Reprinted by permission of Random House, Inc.)

16. Action for Children's Television. ACT petitions Federal Trade Commission, *ACT NEWSLETTER*, Spring/Summer 1972.

17. Kupferberg, H. Your kids need better TV—you can help. *Parade Magazine, Long Island Press,* January 30, 1972.

18. ACT press release, July 18, 1972.

19. Jennings, R. *Programming and advertising practices in television directed to children.* Boston: Action for Children's Television, 1970.

20. Milton Bradley Company 1969 Annual Report.

21. Reach kids on adult TV shows; it's cheaper on kid's shows; Curtis conference on advertising for children brings heated exchanges. *Advertising Age*, July 19, 1965.

22. *Broadcasting*, June 30, 1969.

23. Barcus, F. E. Description of children's television advertising. Paper presented at the meeting of the Federal Trade Commission. Hearings on Modern Advertising Practices, November 19, 1971.

24. Shayon, R. Caveat pre-emptor, *Saturday Review*, January 9, 1971.

25. Ward, S., Levinson, D., & Wackman, D. Children's attention to television advertising. In E. A. Rubinstein, G. A. Comstock, and J. P. Murray (eds.). *Television and social behavior. Vol. IV: Television in day-to-day life: Patterns of use.* Washington, D. C.: U.S. Government Printing Office, 1972, pp. 491–515.

26. Blatt, J., Spencer, L., & Ward, S. A cognitive developmental study of children's reactions to television advertising. In E. A. Rubinstein, G. A. Comstock, and J. P. Murray (eds.). *Television and social behavior. Vol. IV: Television in day-to-day life: Patterns of use.* Washington, D.C.: U.S. Government Printing Office, 1972, pp. 452–467.

27. Ward, S., Reale, G., & Levinson, D. Children's perceptions, explanations, and judgments of television advertising: A further exploration. In E. A. Rubinstein, G. A. Comstock, and J. P. Murray (eds.). *Television and social behavior. Vol. IV: Television in day-to-day life: Patterns of use.* Washington, D.C.: U.S. Government Printing Office, 1972, pp. 468–490.

28. Ward, S. & Wackman, D. Television advertising and intrafamily influence: Children's purchase influence attempts and parental yielding. In E. A Rubinstein, G. A. Comstock, and J. P. Murray (eds.). *Television and social behavior. Vol. IV: Television in day-to-day life: Patterns of use.* Washington D.C.: U.S. Government Printing Office, 1972, pp. 516–525.

8

CONTROL OF CONTENT:
THE GOVERNMENT AND THE INDUSTRY

CONDITIONS ATTACHED TO LICENSES:...the Commission shall determine that public interest, convenience, and necessity would be served by the granting of a license to broadcast.

REVOCATION OF LICENSES: Any station license may be revoked because of conditions...which would warrant the Commission in refusing to grant a license on a original application. . . .

Public Law No. 416.
The Communications Act of 1934

Television is a complex institution. We are concerned primarily with its psychological and cultural effects on children, but to complete our study we must consider television's interaction with politics and the law. This chapter, on the regulation of television, is included because these issues naturally influence the possibilities for change.

THE FCC

The Federal Communications Commission is a government body which regulates broadcasting in the United States. Established by the Communications Act of 1934, its major initial function was to grant licenses to stations to broadcast in particular geographic locales. Built into this function is some power for regulation; the agency can revoke licenses, which must be renewed every 3 years. But its potential for assuring that TV offerings are in the public interest has not been used effectively. Although certain program categories are recommended to licensees by the FCC, the agency makes no attempt to determine what will go into them. While it has revoked licenses (WLBT in Jackson, Mississippi was denied renewal because it presented negative stories about the city's large black community), the FCC's active decisions are politically motivated — and rare.

One justification for the FCC's inaction has its basis in a *laissez-faire* stance regarding government control, as exemplified by former Commissioner Lee Loevinger's words[1].

> *The establishment of renewal roulette in the broadcasting field will certainly destroy any semblance of free press and free speech in the broadcasting media. . . . What degree of freedom or independence can exist for an enterprise which is wholly dependent upon the favor and whim of a government agency for its existence at intervals of not more than three years?* (p. 385)

Today the industry is very far from being the FCC's pawn; in fact, almost the reverse is true. Consider a case in point. In 1963, Newton Minow, then FCC Commissioner, proposed that public hearings be held on the problem of overcommercialism. The FCC debated between regulating on a case by case basis or formulating a general rule. It finally decided to take the latter course, and announced that stations would have to adhere to rules stated in the television code of the National Association of Broadcasters. This seemed like a reasonable procedure, since the government would thereby impose only those standards formulated by the industry itself[2].

Remarkably, the NAB opposed the plan of using its own code and actually organized committees in each state to lobby against it[1]. Such a move, the broadcasters felt, would have set a dangerous precedent leading perhaps to further enforcement of what appears to be just a public relations document never intended to guide actual practices. The Code states in part:

> *Television is seen and heard in every type of American home. These homes include children and adults of all ages, embrace all races and all varieties of religious faith, and reach those of every educational background. It is the responsibility of television to bear constantly in mind that the audience is primarily a home audience, and consequently that television's relationship to the viewers is that between guest and host. . . . By law the television broadcaster is responsible for the programming of his station. He,*

however, is obligated to bring his positive responsibility for excellence and good taste in programming to bear upon all who have a hand in the production of programs, including networks, sponsors, producers of film and of live programs, advertising agencies, and talent agencies. . . .

Television and all who participate in it are jointly accountable to the American public for respect for the special needs of children, for community responsibility, for the advancement of education and culture, for the acceptability of the program materials chosen, for decency and decorum in production, and for propriety in advertising. This responsibility cannot be discharged by any given group of programs, but can be discharged only through the highest standards of respect for the American home, applied to every moment of every program presented by television.

In order that television programming may best serve the public interest, viewers should be encouraged to make their criticisms and positive suggestions known to the television broadcasters. Parents in particular should be urged to see to it that out of the richness of television fare, the best programs are brought to the attention of their children. . . .

The presentation of techniques of crime in such detail as to invite imitation shall be avoided . . . violence and illicit sex shall not be presented in an attractive manner, nor to an extent such as will lead a child to believe that they play a greater part in life than they do.

Racial or nationality types shall not be shown on television in such a manner as to ridicule the race or nationality.

Television broadcasters should exercise the utmost care and discrimination with regard to advertising material, including content, placement and presentation, near or adjacent to programs designed for children. No considerations of expediency should be permitted to impinge upon the vital responsibility towards children and adolescents, which is inherent in television, and which must be recognized and accepted by all advertisers employing television.

Before the FCC could hold hearings on the NAB's system, the Subcommittee on Communications and Power of the House Committee on Interstate and Foreign Commerce approved a bill prohibiting FCC control. By that time (February 1964), the FCC had gained a new member who also opposed the plan and cast the deciding vote against it[2].

Why is the FCC not more successful even when it does bid for regulation? Again, at least a partial answer lies in the political realm. The agency has not been reticent to play favorites. From 1948 to 1952, for example, a freeze on new station licenses was in effect because of war restrictions and many citizens—and business people—were eager to jump on the TV bandwagon. Then, in late 1952, the freeze was lifted; among the first cities to get a station was Austin, Texas, when KTBC-TV was licensed—to Mrs. Lyndon B. Johnson.

On the other side of the coin, broadcasters hold implicit (or explicit) power over politicians; they may decide to "give" a congressman time on the air to report to his district, or to endorse or support his candidacy for reelection. Politicians who are "anti-broadcasting" in their dealings with the FCC are unlikely to enjoy this largesse.

The Great Cigarette War

Perhaps the clearest demonstration of the inseparability of politics and the regulation of television by the FCC is the story of the demise of cigarette commercials on television. Thomas Whiteside, writing for *The New Yorker*, provides a brief history of a long debate[3].

Television had been as effective for the cigarette advertiser as for the toy manufacturer—sales of Benson & Hedges 100's rose from about $1\frac{1}{2}$ billion cigarettes in 1966 to over 14 billion in 1970, following an amusing and sophisticated television campaign. The television industry was pleased with its highly lucrative arrangement with cigarette manufacturers—it took in over 200 millions dollars each year in revenue, accounting for 8–10% of the commercials, or 80 minutes per week[4]. Not surprisingly, neither group was particularly interested in any move that might damage the relationship.

The first blow was struck in June 1967, when the FCC ruled that the "Fairness Doctrine" (that both sides of a controversial issue be given equal time) applied to cigarette advertising. The FCC suggested that a ratio of three cigarette commercials to every one anti-smoking commercial was fair. During the summer, about a dozen petitions were filed on behalf of ABC, NBC, CBS, the National Association of Broadcasters, over 100 individual radio and television stations, six major tobacco companies, the Tobacco Institute, and Federal Communications Bar Association, each asking for revocation of the regulation. John Banzhaf

III, who had originally requested that anti-smoking commercials be aired, asked various health organizations to assist in preparing a reply to these petitions. According to Banzhaf, one official remarked, "Let me tell you the economic facts of life. My organization depends on free broadcasting time for our fund-raising drives. We are not going to jeopardize that time by getting involved in this move"[3] (p. 48). So Banzhaf prepared the brief personally, and was successful. The FCC upheld its ruling in September 1967.

But enforcement was another matter. The FCC had a staff of only four persons to monitor about 1000 TV and 7000 radio stations. Since the Commission clearly could not handle the load, Banzhaf again decided to do it himself. With the help of friends, he watched prime time television for 2 weeks on one large station, WNBC-TV in New York. His monitoring revealed a ratio of cigarette commercials to anti-smoking commercials of 10 to 1; the station said the ratio was 3 or 4 to 1. The discrepancy was due to the fact that WNBC counted two cigarette commercials, one right after another, as one, and did not count simple announcements ("This show is brought to you by Marlboro") at all. Also, the anti-smoking ads were aired at what might be considered by most standards rather odd hours — 2:30 a.m., 6:30 a.m. (WNBC-TV defended the 6:30 a.m. ads, explaining that it wanted to reach the kids before they left for school). Banzhaf's work resulted in the FCC requiring more anti-smoking ads.

Then in 1969, the agency signaled its intention to call for a total ban on cigarette ads. Congress opened special hearings to consider such a bill. Testimony revealed contradictions in the NAB television code and its practices. The TV code calls for cigarette ads which do not present smoking as an activity to be imitated, but a private study by the NAB indicated that many commercials did just that, making smoking appear attractive and socially desirable. The industry preferred to ignore that study. In 1968, the Director of NAB said, "Network [affiliates] . . . see in the area of cigarette copy nothing to be achieved by Code Authority involvement and in fact [see] potential injury to cigarette-advertising revenue if the Code Authority pursues such a course."[3] (p. 70) In the end, after vigorous lobbying by both the tobacco and the broadcasting industries, the House passed a bill which would prevent federal and state intervention for 6 years.

Chances for the bill's passage in the Senate did not appear favorable, so both the networks and the tobacco industry began to offer compromise plans. The networks offered to gradually fade out advertising of brands with the highest tar and nicotine content; this plan was rejected. The broadcasters then suggested that they would phase out advertising over a 3½-year period, beginning in January 1970. The tobacco industry offered another plan: a promise to end all radio and television advertising by September 1970. In return, it hoped to win legislation which would prevent the Federal Trade Commission from requiring health warnings in all ads. This plan rather annoyed the broadcasters (who would lose an additional 3 years of advertising revenue) and one commented[3]:

> The thing that irks us is that the tobacco people couldn't have got the bill through the House without our help. We really lobbied for that. It would never have passed the House without us, because we have more muscle than the tobacco people have.... In every congressman's district, there is at least one broadcaster. These congressmen all get exposure on the local TV and radio stations. ...I know how hard we worked through our local broadcasters on this bill, pointing out to congressmen how unfair it was to bar advertising for a product legally sold.... (p. 78)

The tobacco industry had advertising contracts with the stations; they asked that the contracts be broken. The networks refused. Finally, a bill was proposed to ban cigarette ads on TV after January 1, 1971, giving the networks the ad revenues from the lucrative football season. The Public Health Cigarette Smoking Act was passed by both the House and the Senate and signed into law by President Nixon on April 1, 1970. The last cigarette commercial was shown on January 1, 1971.

This incident in the history of broadcasting points out clearly the array of political influences which underlies regulation of television programming. More specifically, it demonstrates that while the FCC is capable of carrying out a regulatory function, it requires impetus from the outside (e.g., Banzhaf's group)[5].

THE FTC

Recent complaints about television commercials have focused on advertising content, bringing the issue into the domain of the Federal Trade Commission. Beginning in the area of fraudulent and deceptive advertising, the FTC attempted to acquire documentation of all claims made for products.

Preliminary analysis of the project indicates that it is less than a complete success[6]. During the first 9 months, 30% of the documentation was simply inadequate. For example, 13 gasoline mileage claims could not be evaluated because the tests were run by professional drivers under strict driving conditions instead of by average drivers under normal conditions. Another 30% of the reports were so technical that the average consumer would not have understood them. Almost half of the auto makers' reports fell into this category.

The FTC's investigations have revealed some interesting information, however, about the deception prevalent in many advertisements[6]. One ad for a major shaving cream demonstrated that its product gives a cleaner shave; the commercial showed the shaving cream being spread on sandpaper, and then being whisked off perfectly. The FTC claimed that this could not be accomplished unless the sandpaper was soaked for an hour; in fact, it was done even more neatly, by "shaving" sand off a pane of glass! In another incredible display, a major automobile manufacturer demonstrated the clarity of its window glass—with the windows rolled down.

Although most advertisers are not guilty of such blatantly deceptive techniques, many do make extravagant claims which they cannot meet. The usual first step of the FTC is to send the offender a cease and desist order. Many companies respond positively to these orders: after one, Listerine was no longer promoted as a deterrent to colds (which it is not). The FTC filed complaints concerning Dristan and Allerest because these products do not completely prevent or alleviate allergies as their ads suggested (Dristan ads said, "Do anything you darn well please without worrying about hay fever miseries," and "Now I can even chew on ragweed"). Both companies signed consent agreements and changed their commercials. Most altercations over commercials, 75%, are resolved in this manner. Cease and desist orders are not always effective, however. After the Geritol company persisted in advertising its product as a cure for "tired blood," the FTC finally sued for 1 million dollars. That brought results.

With a cease and desist order, although the old ad disappears, the public is never informed of the reason, and no redress is offered to consumers who were influenced by the misleading ad. Two additional courses of action have therefore been suggested: the class action suit and the counter advertisement. The class action suit permits a handful of individuals to sue for damages on behalf of a large class of consumers; it is valuable because few individuals who paid $1 for a product are going to sue the company by themselves. The counter advertisement presents information that refutes claims of commercials; it is based on the principle of the fairness doctrine that was invoked in the case of cigarette advertising. Consumer and environmental agencies now are suggesting counter advertisements to commercials for drug products (like pain-killers) and automobiles, which they claim encourage drug abuse and pollution[7]. The FTC agrees, and in January 1970 proposed that broadcasters be required to air rebuttals to commercials which deal with "issues of current public importance." This suggestion is now in the hands of the FCC, which can actually authorize such policy.

In the meantime, broadcasters and advertisers are fighting the concept tooth and nail, arguing that "issues of public concern" can include just about any ad that implicitly expresses a point of view. Thus, almost every advertiser could be open to counter commercials. The advertisers are unlikely to lay themselves open in this way—they are more likely to take their money to newspapers and magazines, which eventually could lead to the demise of commercial television. Julian Goodman, president of NBC, argues: "The possibility of forced counter-commercials would reduce the medium's advertising effectiveness to the point of undermining its whole economic base."[7] (p. 66) That might or might not be a good thing, but a more serious charge has been leveled at counter advertisers: they are not required to document their claims in the way the FTC now requires of ordinary advertisers. Nevertheless, counter commercials, encouraged by deceptive advertising, may be appearing more often in the future.

SELF-REGULATION BY THE INDUSTRY

The NAB

We have already mentioned that the industry itself, embodied in the National Association of Broadcasters, has a television code pertinent to a number of aspects of television programming. All three major networks, and about two-thirds of the nation's stations subscribe to it[8]. Recall, though, that they were opposed to government enforcement of the code and blatantly violate almost every one of its articles. Indeed, the NAB would hardly be able to impose these restrictions on its own members, even if it chose to try; it has virtually no power[9].

> *The only formal sanction which the NAB may impose upon a subscriber is denial of authorization to display the NAB seal of good practice ... the NAB's provisions for confidential proceedings on possible code violations and its failure to make any provision for*

publicizing violations keeps industry practices out of the public limelight, thus further weakening the Association's powers to effect changes and improvements. (p. 601)

The NAB has not used even its symbolic power of revoking the seal of good practice in nearly 10 years[8].

The television code authority staff is supposed to review programs and interpret the code. They are severely limited; the New York office has only thirteen employees, including secretarial help. It is, therefore, virtually impossible for the authority to monitor the tremendous volume of programming as it occurs. CBS has resisted the alternative suggestion that programs be prescreened, but ABC and NBC have begun to submit pilots of new series to the authority prior to the new season. None of the networks, though, submits each episode of each series[8].

The Network Censors

In practice, regulation of television content is carried out by employees of each network, the censors. The media task force of the National Commission on the Causes and Prevention of Violence examined the efforts of the three networks to conform to their own versions of the NAB code[9].

It interviewed censors and various other network officials, and obtained the censors' previously written comments about twenty-six episodes of several series on each network. The task force noted, however, that time did not permit comparing the censors' suggestions with the program which was finally aired, a procedure which might have been most instructive, since the censors' instructions are often not followed[9].

ABC

The major concern of ABC is that the audience not be shocked. The literature on the effects of television on children and adults, available at the time the media task force conducted its investigation, was not considered helpful in determining television content. In an interview, an ABC official revealed four specific criteria for evaluating television violence:

1. no sensationalism merely to attract audience;
2. concern and awareness of the public's feelings;
3. questions of public taste;
4. desire not to generate a negative reaction in viewers. (p. 602)

Examination of some specific comments made by the censors may be helpful. The following instructions were found in documents relating to the series *Guns of Will Sonnet*:

> *This beating of the sick boy is too sadistic and must be modified — to one blow — certainly not so vicious or so prolonged as described.*

> *Caution on the appearance of dead bodies. Keep blood to a minimum and the eyes closed, please. Caution. Do not overdo, re: display of blood here.*

> *No close-ups of arrows piercing Milt's back or Dan's chest — and nothing too gruesome for audience in subsequent scenes, re: Dan's appearance.* (pp. 602–603)

The following comments and instructions were made in regard to various episodes of the series *The Avengers*:

> *In order not to repel too many viewers, the business with Grant and the boa constrictor will have to be handled with a minimum of close-ups of the snake and avoidance of shots showing it in contact with the man. When final struggle is on — his movements, moans, and facial expressions can only be approved after screening unless avoided for the most part.*

> *Keep shots of snakes as distant and unrepulsive as possible.*

> *Benstead's electrocution must not be too brutal for home viewing.*

> *Gifford's screams should be kept to a minimum.* (p. 603)

ABC does make some attempts to consider the potential effects of its programming as can be seen from the following admonitions relating to *Felony Squad*:

> *Special caution that we do not demonstrate exactly how the fire is set; the chemicals being mixed not identified; in the scenes of the bug "working" — please suggest what he is doing rather than graphically detailing same.*

> *Caution that, in script development, we do not reveal or give a demonstration of arson techniques, by action or dialogue, so as to invite imitation.*

> *Please modify and keep action coverage so that we do not show how the "torch" is made and possibly invite imitation.* (p. 603)

NBC

Regarding the treatment of violence, NBC's code provides:

> *Whether in terms of human conflict or cruelty to animals, violence should never be presented for its own sake, for shock effect or as an audience stimulant and should never be carried to excess. Depictions of violence can be justified as an expression of conflict only to the extent essential to the advancement of plot or the depiction of characterization.* (p. 604)

Comments on the program *High Chaparral* will serve as an example of the censorship of NBC programs. Among the most frequent cautions were:

1. Avoid excessive bloodiness of wounds (there were a total of 21 cautions in 26 programs).
2. Delete the impact of the instrument of aggression, bullet, arrow, gun butt, etc. (a total of 32 instances where the impact was deleted or softened by showing it out of frame or moved off camera).
3. Fights are not to be unnecessarily long or brutal.
4. Victims of homicide are to be shown with their eyes closed and not positioned grotesquely. (p. 605)

In addition to these general comments the censorship department of NBC has more specific recommendations. The producers were urged to:

1. Eliminate any suggestion of sadism:
   It is felt by this department that one blast from BUCK's shotgun is sufficient to stop CLEEG. Therefore, it is unnecessary for BUCK to fire both barrels which would lead our viewers into believing BUCK to be a sadistic killer.
2. Avoid brutality:
   Please find another means for MANOLETO to knock the knife from CARLO's hand instead of MANOLETO kicking him somewhere below the beltline.
3. Eliminate excessive violence:
   The killing of RICARDO is acceptable; however, the killing of the other RURALES we feel, is excessive and unnecessary. Please find some other way of dispatching them without killing them.
   CURRY slugging BLUE seems to be unnecessary as he has

already clubbed him with his revolver. One or the other is acceptable, but not both.

4. Avoid showing the misery, or consequences of violence:

   Take care that the scene with an arrow jutting from ANNALEE's breast is not done in a shocking or objectionable manner.

   Caution on MANOLETO's killing RINALDO with the scythe.

   Please use off-camera technique in showing BLUE taking the thorns from underneath the nails of the tortured Indian.

   Please avoid any close-up exposure of the dead body of BURNS pierced with arrows.

   As the kid is shot and he starts to fall, please avoid sensationalizing his fall as he goes tumbling down the rocks. It will be unacceptable to see the kid bouncing from rock to rock in his fall.

   As MARIA cradles the dying RAMON in her arms, avoid showing the knife protruding from RAMON's chest.

5. Avoid scenes likely to terrorize children:

   Please avoid prolonging or sensationalizing these scenes whereby ANGIE is trapped by the coiled rattlesnake. The child can be frightened but not terrorized by her dilemma.

6. Ensure that the overall moral tone of the story remains in accord with the NAB standards:

   On page 11 it is felt by this department that the pistol-whipping of the doctor's patient PEDRO is unnecessary. PEDRO can just be knocked cold to achieve the same effect. The ending as presently written is unacceptable to this department; there must be some retribution for DOC's kidnapping and extortion. He just can't ride off scot free. (pp. 605–606)

CBS

CBS appears to take more care and be more concerned about the presentation of violence in both adult and children's programming than the other networks, and Gerbner found CBS to be the least violent of the networks[8]. This is only a relative statement, though, as the examples below suggest.

The head of CBS standards and practices stated in an interview that "the nearest thing the network has to an expressed standard is that the network shall present as little violence as possible without interfering with the creative process." One of the programs studied by the media task force was *The Wild, Wild West*. Typical cautions in the handling of violence include:

1. Excessive violence:
   It is understood that rather than a fusillade, only two arrows will strike the Digger, and that this will be handled with appropriate caution.

   To avoid hitting the attendant, we suggest that West employ the pressure point gimmick.

   We ask that West and Artemus sneak past the guard rather than have West knock him out.

   Artemus should not shoot more than two of the deputies on camera.

2. Shortening the length or brutality of fights.
   The fight between West and O'Reilly should not be excessively long or brutal.

   Please exercise directorial caution in filming of the fights to prevent brutality or excessive length.

3. Eliminate traces of sadism:
   To avoid any element of sadism, caution should be exercised in showing Enrique and the prisoner seen hanging in Sordo's camp.

4. Avoid grotesque positioning of dead bodies:
   O'Reilly's . . . body should not be displayed in a grotesque manner [after he falls from the ledge].

5. Soften or do not show consequences of horror of violence:
   It is our understanding the shot will be cut away as soon as Freemandle falls into vat [of acid].

   We should not see the mace imbedded in his back as indicated.

   We trust appropriate caution will be exercised in the make-up of the bloody Cassidy. Make-up caution should be exercised when showing the dead man. Obviously his being shown with "his skull neatly caved in" [as the script called for] is unacceptable.

6. Restraint vis-à-vis women:
   Please delete scenes of the restrained girl being slapped. Suggest only sound of slap before assumed shot of Dorcas, and in place of second slap she be shaken, or be threatened with a second slap.

7. Do not shock or frighten the audience:
   To prevent morbidity, we ask that the coffin not be seen burning.

   To prevent shock or horror, the business of Draja removing his iron hand not be detailed or emphasized. The wounded Benje should not howl in pain as indicated.

In Sum

The media task force summarized their findings of the networks presentation of violence:

> *Present network standards on portrayals of violence are weak because they appear to be based on little more than a fear of losing viewers. Little consideration is given to the issue of whether violence is indeed necessary to maintain dramatic tension in the resolution of conflict, and only cursory attention is paid to the larger question of reducing the number of violent programs in network entertainment schedules.* (p. 613)

CONGRESSIONAL INQUIRIES INTO TV VIOLENCE

As early as 1954, Senator Estes Kefauver, then Chairman of the Senate Subcommittee on Juvenile Delinquency, questioned the need for violent content on television entertainment. Network representatives claimed at that time that research on the effects of violence viewing upon children was inconclusive, although they admitted that some risk existed. In addition, Harold E. Fellows, President and Chairman of the Board of the National Association of Broadcasters, promised that the NAB would undertake research on the impact of television programming on children.

The Dodd Hearings

In 1961, Senator Thomas Dodd, then chairman of the same subcommittee, inquired about violence on children's television. Testimony during hearings revealed that the television industry's use of violence had remained both rampant and opportunistic[10].

> *An independent producer was asked to "inject an 'adequate' diet of violence into scripts" ... Another network official wrote 'I like the idea of sadism.' ... 'Give me sex and action' demanded one executive.* (p. 40)

Also it was clear that the previously promised research had not been carried out. Leroy Collins, the new president of the NAB explained[9]:

> *Soon [after Mr. Fellows' testimony] the television code review board undertook a pilot study of "viewer attitudes" to determine*

the feasibility of a broader study, but about that time the Columbia Broadcasting System announced that it was engaged in sponsoring a survey which, while broader, would cover essentially the same ground. In view of this overlapping inquiry, NAB deferred to CBS in order that the larger survey could go ahead in preference to the narrower inquiry which the NAB had initiated. It is anticipated that the CBS project will be completed by the end of this summer [1961] and that a final report will be published before the end of this year. (pp. 593–594)

The report in question was published in 1963 by Gary Steiner[11]. The title, *The People Look at Television*, indicates clearly the subject matter of the volume: the attitudes and beliefs of parents and other viewers about the effects of television on children, not the actual effects as determined by scientific investigation.

But the earlier hearings did have an impact, which one observer described this way[12]:

[The subcommittee staff for the 1961 Dodd hearings] noted that many network series mentioned in early testimony as especially violent were being syndicated, and shown on independent stations throughout the country. One committee aide observed: "It's as if they used our 1961 hearings as a shopping list!" Many of the programs were scheduled at earlier hours than before, and were reaching younger audiences. (p. 203)

In 1961, industry spokesmen again promised more research[9].

. . . we are moving significantly in this area [of research on effects of television on children] now. At a meeting of our joint radio and television board of directors last week approval was given to proceed with the initial planning of an NAB research and training center in association with one of the leading universities in the nation. (p. 594)

James T. Aubrey and Frank Stanton, executives of CBS, as well as executives of NBC and ABC agreed to participate in industry-wide research.

In 1962, the industry co-sponsored the Joint Committee for Research on Television and Children, along with the United States Department of Health, Education and Welfare. This committee, which consisted almost entirely of network personnel, solicited research proposals from various members of the scientific community. Unfortunately, it became clear in

1964 that few of these proposals were being carried out. In fact, only three papers were even begun as a result of the work of the joint committee. The first, by Dr. Ruth Hartley, constituted a criticism and analysis of the inadequacies of research which was detrimental to the industry, not an investigation of the actual effects[13]. A second was conducted by Dr. Seymour Feshbach, a leading proponent of the catharsis hypothesis[14]. The third study was not even completed.

In 1964, as Senator Dodd's hearings continued, network executives again promised to do more research. By this time the excuses had become rather pathetic. When asked by Dodd what had been done, NBC Executive Vice President Walter D. Scott replied this way[9]:

> *I have asked the same question, Senator, because I have wondered why there has not been more in the way of results up to this point. I have been reminded by our people who are working very actively and closely with the Committee that it is appropriate to bear in mind that the work of scholars frequently sets its own pace and that time may be the price we must pay for meaningful results. As I understand it, they have had work done by a very large number of competent scholars in the field of social sciences. I understand that there have been something like one hundred separate projects that have been studied, that these have been narrowed down, that they are now at the stage of being ready to go ahead with, I believe, either five or six specific projects, out of which they hope to get some meaningful answers.* (p. 595)

No new research was ever published or reported by the Committee. Scott went on to become NBC's board chairman.

The Violence Commission

In 1968, the National Commission on the Causes and Prevention of Violence held hearings on the role of the mass media. Once again, network executives were questioned about the promised research; once again, it was not forthcoming. By this time, the networks were arguing that *they* should not be doing research anyway. One ABC executive stated[9]:

> *Research should be done from an objective standpoint and one that the public would be satisfied with as being done objectively, rather than that which is directly financed by our particular company.* (p. 598)

The networks evidently felt no responsibility to determine the effects of television for their own use in determining program content.

Network executives also suggested that research was impossible due to the lack of adequate research design. Dr. Frank Stanton, then president of CBS and himself a Ph.D. psychologist, remarked[9]:

> It isn't unwillingness on the part of the industry to underwrite the research. It is that no one in the thirty-odd years I have been in the business has come up with a technique or methodology that would let you get a fix on this impact.... These people from the outside [of the industry] have been given every encouragement, every funding they have asked for to come up with methodology, and this is the field that is very illusive [sic] and it doesn't do any good to spend a lot of money and come up with facts somebody can punch his fingers through. (p. 598)

Less than 2 years later "people from the outside" funded by the Federal government had come up with a number of research plans which did permit "a fix on this impact." It was possible all along.

The Surgeon General's NIMH Inquiry

In 1969, Senator John O. Pastore, Chairman of the Senate Subcommittee on Communications of the Senate Commerce Committe sent a letter to Health, Education, and Welfare Secretary Robert Finch, which said in part[15]:

> I am exceedingly troubled by the lack of any definitive information which would help resolve the question of whether there is a causal connection between televised crime and violence and antisocial behavior of individuals, especially children.... I am respectfully requesting that you direct the Surgeon General to appoint a committee comprised of distinguished men and women from whatever professions and disciplines deemed appropriate to devise techniques and to conduct a study under his supervision using those techniques which will establish scientifically insofar as possible what harmful effects, if any, these programs have on children.

Secretary Finch directed Surgeon General William H. Stewart to select a committee to authorize and examine evidence relevant to questions about the effects of television on children. The Surgeon General, announcing that he would appoint an advisory panel of scientists respected by the scientific community, the broadcasting industry, and the general public, requested nominations from various academic and professional associations (including the American Sociological Association, the American Anthropological Association, the American Psychiatric Association, and the American Psychological Association), distinguished social scientists, the NAB and the three major networks. From the many names suggested, the office of the Surgeon General drew up a list of 40, and sent it to the presidents of the National Association of Broadcasters and of the three national commercial broadcast networks. The broadcasters were asked to indicate "which individuals, if any, you would believe would *not* be appropriate for an impartial scientific investigation of this nature." They responded with a list of seven names:

Leo Bogart, executive vice president and general manager of the Bureau of Advertising of the American Newspaper Publishers Association. Dr. Bogart had previously published a book on television.

Albert Bandura, professor of psychology at Stanford, and an internationally acknowledged expert on children's imitative learning. Bandura, now president-elect of the American Psychological Association, had published numerous research articles which demonstrated that children can learn to be more aggressive from watching TV.

Leonard Berkowitz, Vilas professor of psychology at the University of Wisconsin, principal investigator of an extensive series of studies showing that watching aggression can stimulate aggressive behavior. Author of two books on aggression, Berkowitz served as a consultant to the 1969 Task Force on Mass Media and Violence.

Leon Eisenberg, professor and chairman of the Department of Psychiatry at Harvard University.

Ralph Garry, then professor of educational psychology at Boston University, author of a book on children's television, and a principal consultant to the U.S. Senate Subcommittee on Juvenile Delinquency. He is now at the Ontario Institute for Studies in Education.

Otto Larsen, professor of sociology at the University of Washington and editor of *Violence and the mass media*.

Percy H. Tannenbaum, then professor of psychology and communication at the University of Pennsylvania, and prominent for his theoretical analyses of the arousing effects of media entertainment depicting violence and sex. He has recently been appointed professor in the Graduate School of Public Policy, University of California at Berkeley.

While these distinguished men were blackballed, the industry secured 5 of the 12 positions for its own executives and consultants. They were:

Thomas Coffin, vice president of NBC
Ira H. Cisin, CBS consultant
Joseph T. Klapper, director of CBS social research
Harold Mendelsohn, CBS consultant
Gerhart D. Wiebe, former CBS executive

This odd selection procedure, of systematic inclusion and exclusion, was not intended to be a matter of the public record. Even the non-network members of the committee, all of whom are well respected by the scientific community, were not told anything about it. When the procedure was uncovered by Stanford professor Edwin Parker and Senator Lee Metcalf, HEW Secretary Robert Finch tried to explain away the travesty as handily as he could, saying that the selection was designed to assure impartiality. James J. Jenkins, then chairman of the American Psychological Association's board of professional affairs, took a different view. He described the procedure as deplorable and analogized[16]:

It looks like an exemplar of the old story of the "regulatees" running the "regulators" or the fox passing on the adequacy of the eyesight of the man assigned to guard the chicken coop. (pp. 951–952)

It is important, though, that the Committee was not directly involved in the commissioning of new research. Instead, 1 million dollars was made available for support of independent projects through the National Institute of Mental Health. About 40 formal proposals were submitted. They were then reviewed by *ad hoc* panels of prominent scientists who were not themselves members of the Committee (by then known as the Surgeon General's Scientific Advisory Committee on Television and Social Behavior). Twenty-three projects were selected and funded in this way; the investigators were free to proceed with their contracted research without interference, and to prepare technical research reports of their findings and of any conclusions they deemed appropriate.

The Advisory Committee Report

Prior to the publication of the individual investigators' reports* the committee reviewed them, as well as previous research, and submitted a report to the Surgeon General. The post had changed hands since the project began, having passed to Jesse Steinfeld who released both a brief summary, as well as the Committee's full report in January 1972.

Although indicating that a causal relationship between violence viewing and aggression by the young had been found, the Committee report was unfortunately worded so as to lead to misunderstanding, and the summary was flatly misleading. One journalist, Jack Gould of the *New York Times*, wrote a "scoop" story of the report with the headline, "TV Violence Held Unharmful to Youth."[17]

The Committee's hedging may or may not have been predictible, given its diverse composition and the political pressure to produce a unanimously signed document. At any rate, the private goings on were surely not dull. According to John P. Murray, research coordinator for the project and one of the few non-Committee members who was present during the deliberations[18]:

> *There was a big move by Government officials to get a consensus report. There was a lot of anger, the meetings were extremely tense with the warring factions sitting at either end of the table, glaring at each other, particularly toward the end.* (p. 28)

The result was undoubtedly a compromise, with the "network five" scoring its share in the battle. According to *Newsweek*, in a story "correcting" its earlier interpretation[19]:

> *At one point during the committee meetings ... former CBS consultant Wiebe raised his eyes from a particularly damning piece of evidence and grumbled: "This looks like it was written by someone who hates television." But the most ardent defender of the industry was CBS research director Joseph Klapper, who lobbied for the inclusion, among other things, of a plethora of "howevers" in the final report.* (p. 55)

Many of the researchers associated with the project felt that their work had been represented inaccurately, at least to the extent of minimizing what seemed a clear relationship between viewing of TV violence and

---

*A complete description of each of the funded projects and of other technical documents associated with the work can be found in Appendix A.

youngsters' aggressive behavior. Dr. Monroe Lefkowitz, Principal Research Scientist at the New York State Department of Mental Hygiene wrote in a letter to Senator Pastore:

> *The Surgeon General's Scientific Advisory Committee on Television and Social Behavior in my opinion ignores, dilutes, and distorts the research findings in their report, "Television and Growing Up: the Impact of Televised Violence." As a contributor of one of the technical reports whose study dealt with television violence and aggressive behavior ... I feel that the Committee's conclusions about the causal nature of television violence in producing aggressive behavior are hedged by erroneous statements, are over-qualified, and are potentially damaging to children and society ...*

Lefkowitz' response is strong, but it is by no means unique. Matilda Paisley, in a report of Stanford University's Institute for Communication Research (*Social policy research and the realities of the system: violence done to TV research*), indicates that fully half of the researchers who replied to her questionnaire stated that the results of their own research had not been adequately reported by the Committee[18]. Some typical replies, with letters substituted for respondents' names, appear below:

> *Respondent B commented that, "In fact, they went too deep on some of our extraneous findings, in order to obscure the main conclusion." Respondents G, L, and P spoke of "strange emphases," "misleading focus," and "selective emphases," respectively. Respondents E and F spoke of errors in reporting their research. Respondent T stated that "the conclusions are diluted and overqualified."* (Appendix III, p. 4)

One item on the Paisley questionnaire read: *Whatever the findings of your own research suggest,* which of the following relationships of violence viewing to aggressiveness do you feel now is the most plausible?*

(a) viewing television violence increases aggressiveness;
(b) viewing television violence decreases aggressiveness;
(c) viewing television violence has no effect on aggressiveness;
(d) the relationship between violence viewing and aggressiveness depends on a third variable or set of variables;
(e) other, please specify?

*Almost half of the investigators were involved in projects which did not bear directly on this question.

None of the 20 investigators who responded to this question selected answer (b); none selected (c). Clearly, then, these researchers felt that there was a relationship between TV violence and aggressiveness, and that the long touted catharsis hypothesis (*see* pp. 44–48) was untenable. Seventy percent of the respondents simply selected response (a): viewing television violence increases aggressiveness. All of the remainder qualified their replies with some version of alternatives (d) or (e).

The Pastore Hearings

In March 1972, shortly after the publication of the technical reports, Senator Pastore held further hearings to clarify the situation[20]. When questioned by Senator Pastore and members of his subcommittee, Ithiel de Sola Pool, a member of the Surgeon General's Advisory Committee, commented:

> *Twelve scientists of widely different views unanimously agreed that scientific evidence indicated that the viewing of television violence by young people causes them to behave more aggressively.* (p. 47)

Alberta Siegel, another Committee member, remarked:

> *Commercial television makes its own contribution to the set of factors that underlie aggressiveness in our society. It does so in entertainment through ceaseless repetition of the message that conflict may be resolved by aggression, that violence is a way of solving problems.* (p. 63)

Pool and Siegel were among the academic members of the Committee; they had pressed for a strong report on the basis of the data all along. But even Ira Cisin, Thomas Coffin, and the other "network" Committee members agreed that the situation was sufficiently serious to warrant some action.

The networks' chief executives also testified. Julian Goodman, President of NBC, stated:

> *We agree with you that the time for action has come. And, of course, we are willing to cooperate in any way together with the rest of the industry.* (p. 182)

Elton H. Rule of the American Broadcasting Company promised:

> *Now that we are reasonably certain that televised violence can increase aggressive tendencies in some children, we will have to manage our program planning accordingly.* (p. 217)

Surgeon General Steinfeld made the unequivocal statement that:

> *Certainly my interpretation is that there is a causative relationship between televised violence and subsequent antisocial behavior, and that the evidence is strong enough that it requires some action on the part of responsible authorities, the TV industry, the Government, the citizens.* (p. 28)

Although few social scientists would put the seal "Absolutely Proven" on this, or any other body of research, the weight of the evidence and the outcry of the news media did become sufficient to produce a belated recognition of the implications of the research. Testimony and documentation at the Hearings of the Subcommittee on Communications, U.S. Senate, were overwhelming. Senator Pastore now had his answer. It is captured entirely in the following interchange, late in the hearings, between Pastore and Dr. Eli Rubinstein. (Rubinstein was Vice-Chairman of the Surgeon General's Committee and, in Dr. Steinfeld's absence, monitored the research and refereed the Committee.)

> *SENATOR PASTORE.   And you are convinced, like the Surgeon General, that we have enough data now [about the effects of television on children] to take action?*
>
> *DR. RUBINSTEIN.   I am, sir.*
>
> *SENATOR PASTORE.   Without a re-review. It will only substantiate the facts we already know. Irrespective of how one or another individual feels, the fact still remains that you are convinced, as the Surgeon General is convinced, that there is a causal relationship between violence on television and social behavior on the part of children?*
>
> *DR. RUBINSTEIN.   I am, sir.*
>
> *SENATOR PASTORE.   I think we ought to take it from there. . . .* (p. 152)

But where shall we take it? It is to this question which we turn in the next chapter.

REFERENCES

1. Mayer, M. *About television*. New York: Harper & Row, 1972.
2. Longley, L. D. The FCC's attempt to regulate commercial time. *Journal of Broadcasting*, 1967, **11**, 83–89.
3. Whiteside, T. Annals of advertising. *The New Yorker*, December 19, 1970. pp. 42–48ff.

4. The last drag. *Newsweek*, January 4, 1971, p. 65. (Copyright Newsweek, Inc., 1971. Reprinted by permission.)

5. Minow, N. N. *Equal time: The private broadcaster and the public interest.* New York: Atheneum, 1964. (Copyright © 1964 by Newton N. Minow. Reprinted by permission of Atheneum Publishers.)

6. Henninger, D. The one-eyed sucker. *The New Republic*, May 2, 1970. pp. 17–19.

7. Counter-commercials; movement by public-interest groups under fairness doctrine. *Newsweek*, June 5, 1972, pp. 65–66.

8. Gerbner, G. The structure and process of television program content regulation in the United States. In G. A. Comstock and E. A. Rubinstein (eds.). *Television and social behavior. Vol. I: Media content and control.* Washington, D.C.: U.S. Government Printing Office, 1972, pp. 386–414.

9. Baker, R. K. The views, standards, and practices of the television industry. In R. K. Baker and S. J. Ball (eds.). *Violence and the media.* Washington, D.C.: U.S. Government Printing Office, 1969, pp. 593–614.

10. Johnson, N. *How to talk back to your television set.* Boston: Atlantic-Little, Brown and Company, 1967.

11. Steiner, G. A. *The people look at television.* New York: Alfred A. Knopf, 1963.

12. Barnouw, E. *A History of broadcasting in the United States. Vol. III — from 1953: The image empire.* New York: Oxford University Press, 1972, p. 203. (Copyright © 1972 by Erik Barnouw.)

13. Hartley, R. L. *The impact of viewing "aggression": Studies and problems of extrapolation.* New York: Columbia Broadcasting System Office of Social Research, 1964.

14. Feshbach, S. & Singer, R. *Television and aggression.* San Francisco: Jossey-Bass, 1971.

15. Cisin, I. H., Coffin, T. E., Janis, I. L., Klapper, J. T., Mendelsohn, H., Omwake, E., Pinderhughes, C. A., Pool, I. de Sola, Siegel, A. E., Wallace, A. F. C., Watson, A. S., & Wiebe, G. D. *Television and growing up: The impact of televised violence.* Washington, D.C.: U.S. Government Printing Office, 1972.

16. Boffey, P. M. & Walsh, J. Study of TV violence. Seven top researchers blackballed from panel. *Science*, May 22, 1970, Vol. 168 pp. 949–952. (Copyright © 1970 by The American Association for the Advancement of Science.)

17. Gould, J. TV violence held unharmful to youth. *The New York Times*, January 11, 1972.

18. Paisley, M. B. *Social policy research and the realities of the system: violence done to TV research.* Institute of Communication Research: Stanford University, 1972.

19. Violence revisited. *Newsweek*, March 6, 1972, pp. 55–56. (Copyright Newsweek, Inc. 1972. Reprinted by permission.)

20. U.S. Congress, Senate. Hearings before the subcommittee on Communications of the Committee on Commerce. March 1972.

9

THE PAST—AND THE FUTURE

The question most often asked about children's television, almost from the time of its first appearance, has been, "Does extensive viewing of violence by our youth contribute significantly to the prevalence of violence in our society?" Finding the answer has been costly because each child obviously comes under the influence of many factors and his behavior is determined by a wide array of experiences. This complexity has, on occasion, led some to retreat from the question entirely.

But the real issue is to weigh the evidence in light of the consequences of maintaining and teaching violence. While some quibble, violence continues to become a way of life. The quibbling is unwarranted. On the basis of evaluation of many lines of converging evidence, involving more than 50 studies which have included more than 10,000 normal children and adolescents from every conceivable background, the weight of the evidence is clear: The demonstrated teaching and instigating effects of aggressive television fare upon youth are of sufficient importance to warrant immediate remedial action.

Viewing televised violence is not, of course, the only contributing factor to aggression. Cigarette smoking is by no means the only factor contributing to heart disease; moderate exercise is not the only factor which contributes to good health. But how much influence does any one factor have to show in order to be of social concern and practical importance?

While damaging programming goes unabated, too little is also being

157

made of other evidence—evidence which suggests that programs specifically designed with psychological and educational principles in mind can prove to be highly enjoyable to youngsters while effectively transmitting positive lessons to them and thus producing significant benefits for society.

Even aside from its violent content, United States commercial television for children appears to be the worst in the free world. David Fleiss and Lillian Ambrosino point out, for example, that as of July 1971 only the United States and one other country (Finland) did *not* offer weekday afternoon programs designed especially for children[1]. Nor are

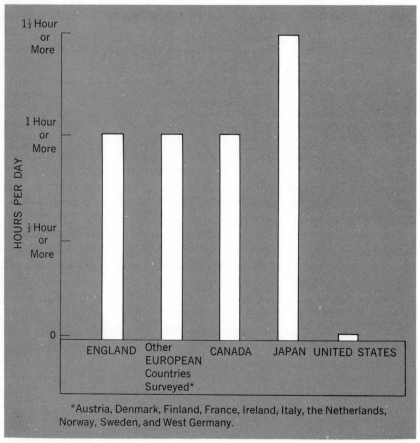

Fig. 9.1   Weekday afternoon nonschool programming for children (Source: Courtesy of National Citizens Committee for Broadcasting).

other nations simply concerned in a "token" way; as seen in Fig. 9.1, the world's average for regular afternoon children's programs, even when school programs are discounted, is more than one full hour per afternoon. So it is clear where we should go from here. Two changes are needed, and long overdue:

1. An immediate and sharp decrease in the amount of violence shown.
2. An equally enthusiastic effort to increase the number of programs designed to teach positive lessons.

How can such changes be brought about?

EXPANDING PROGRAM CHOICE

Public Television

The Carnegie Commission on Educational Television looked to expanding and strengthening educational or "public" television as a way to improved content. In 1967, it issued a report calling for the establishment of a system similar to the British one, but which would finance only educational programming[2]. It also suggested the formation of a trust fund, derived from a tax on the sale of new television receivers (in Britain there is a yearly tax on all television sets), with recommended funding of about 100 million dollars a year.

Instead, the financing for public television has come from annual congressional appropriations to the Corporation for Public Broadcasting. CPB, formed by a 1967 Act of Congress, is an autonomous board of 15 appointed by the President. It is viewed as a service agency to local stations, supplying money for program development. For example, the Public Broadcasting Service, Children's Television Workshop, and the National Educational Television network have all been recipients of grants.

It was assumed that money distributed by CPB would allow the production of quality programs, directed at diverse audiences. The promise has not been fulfilled, in part because of lack of funds. A comparison of program costs for educational and commercial broadcasts, for example, demonstrates the financial handicap of educational TV. E. William Henry[3], former FCC Chairman, reported that in the early 1960s, the average (median) ETV station had about $100,000 per *year* to spend on all its programs; commercial networks often spend the same amount per *half hour*. Money does not guarantee excellence (the commercial networks prove that), but it is a necessary prerequisite; "it's futile to expect brilliance, imagination, artistry, and boldness to be long supported by a bootstrap tied to a shoestring." The success of *Sesame Street,* while clearly traceable to the inspiration of those who developed it, also illustrates the importance of adequate financing. Its shows cost an estimated $50,000 each.

In spite of the apparent need for better funding, increased support for CPB has not received sufficient political backing. In August of 1972, President Nixon vetoed legislation which would have increased the Corporation's funding, alleging that it exercised too much control over local stations. The measure had been overwhelmingly passed in the Congress (259 to 69 in the House and 82 to 1 in the Senate). Critics charged that Nixon's move was clearly politically motivated; Senator Frank Moss of Utah described it as "outrageous." But Congress was forced to come back with a greatly reduced budget in order to assure *any* continued support.

Cable TV

Another possibility for improvement appeared in the expanded use of television involving the development of cable television which allows more channels to be carried, each with a clearer signal than could be obtained from antenna reception. In 1969 the FCC required all cable systems with more than 3500 subscribers to "originate a significant amount of programming." Similarly, in 1971, cable systems serving the top 100 markets were required to offer at least 20 channels to their subscribers. In addition, they must now set aside three channels for noncommercial use: one for education, one for state and local government, and one for public access. The latter can be used on a first come, first served basis with broadcasting costs borne by the user[4].

These recent FCC rulings are significant; previously, cable television had offered little more than standard network fare with some extras, such as sports and movies, thrown in. The new regulations might serve to foster more local programming, such as that currently being offered by the Teleprompter Company in New York City. Teleprompter broadcasts a nightly news show dealing only with northern Manhattan and also broadcasts in Spanish each evening. It shows special documentaries of particular interest to local citizens and originates ten children's shows per week[4].

But the major stumbling block is still money. Cable fees are pocketed by companies who put little money back into the production of new shows. While it may have a desirable impact on increasing the amount of local television, the likelihood of reduced violence on TV or of a rise in mass-oriented quality programs is small.

Thus, it appears that the call for expansion of program offerings through cable or public television does not currently hold much promise for improved television. We must turn to the major networks.

THE POSITION OF THE BROADCASTERS

It has long been hoped by some that voluntary moves by commercial broadcasters would produce change in their programming. In his first public address, FCC Commissioner Newton Minow urged the National Association of Broadcasters[5]:

> *Your license lets you use the public's airwaves as trustees for 180 million Americans. The public is your beneficiary. If you want to stay on as trustees, you must deliver a decent return to the public — not only to your stockholders. So, as a representative of the public, your health and your product are among my chief concerns. As to your health: let's talk only of television today. In 1960 gross broadcast revenues of the television industry were over $1,268,000,000; profit before taxes was $243,900,000 — an average return on revenue of 19.2 percent ... I have confidence in your health. But not in your product .... when television is bad, nothing is worse. I invite you to sit down in front of your television set when your station goes on the air and stay there without a book, magazine, newspaper, profit-and-loss sheet or rating book to distract you — and keep your eyes glued to that set until the station signs off. I can assure you that you will observe a vast wasteland.... Gentlemen, your trust accounting with your beneficiaries is overdue. Never have so few owed so much to so many.*
> (pp. 49–53)

Minow's warning has gone unheeded. Despite recent promises by all three network chiefs to Senator Pastore (*see* p. 154), we cannot be optimistic. Promises for change have often been made in the past — and literally never honored.

In fact, these promises have always existed side by side with the broadcasters' traditional position that a major change in the present system is not warranted — or not necessary. Several specific arguments are often advanced in defense of this position. It is often suggested, for example, that television simply gives the public what it wants. On inspection, this claim involves two points: that television is free — a gift from the broadcasters — and that it merely mirrors public taste.

Is Commercial Television Free?

One common retort of the commercial networks and stations, when challenged about the programming they offer, is that complaints are unfair because television entertainment is made available without cost to the public. Nothing could be further from the truth. The more than 75 million television sets in the United States today involved a total purchase price to viewers of at least 15 billion dollars. An equivalent amount has been spent on their repair and maintenance. The electrical power required to run the sets also represents a substantial figure. Of course, to all this calculation must be added the simple fact that, by buying goods and services advertised on television, it is the consumer who ends up paying for all costs of programs, operation of stations, and the earnings, profits, and investments of the television industry. The 3 billion dollars in net revenues enjoyed by the TV industry last year once belonged to the consumer. Indeed, the Consumers Union pointed out that as of 1960 television viewers — who allegedly were getting something for nothing — had already invested 37 *billion* dollars for television entertainment[6]!

Does Television Merely Reflect Existing Public Taste?

Broadcasters have often claimed that program content is dictated by the pressures of economics and public opinion. The commercialism of TV requires reaching a large audience; audiences are free to tune in or out; thus, the audience controls TV fare. The networks only "give the public what it wants."

Let us examine this argument more closely. First, the networks play a role in training the public to want what they give. One critic has noted[7]:

> As ... mediocrity, which in the short term is economically profitable, fills the air, it creates appetites; it styles the nation's taste just as advertising influences what we eat, smoke and drive. The stock answer of network apologists for the current television schedules is, "We give the people what they want," but what has actually happened is that those viewers who have been brainwashed select their own brand of popcorn, while those of more discerning tastes simply give up watching or listening. ... A Walter Lippmann inter-

view in the weekly time period of Petticoat Junction *would be greeted with just as much outrage as he would receive if you asked him to lecture between the double feature at any of the Forty-second Street movie houses.* (pp. 273–274)

The argument of "audience demand" is flawed on another level as well. It rests on the assumption that the public should get what it wants — regardless. This view may be part and parcel of the long-standing philosophical notion that encourages a wide range of freedoms and diversity among people. Still, a need for some regulation always has been recognized. It is exemplified in the areas of food and drug control.

The case against giving children anything they want is especially clear. As adults we have responsibilities to our children as individuals and as members of society. In their classic *Television in the lives of our children*, Schramm, Lyle, and Parker reviewed an era of television that was less commercialized, and less violence-laden than the present one[8]. Yet TV's offerings, even then, were sufficiently upsetting to lead them to wonder:

Since when has [giving children what they want] become a sufficient doctrine for adult responsibility? Children would doubtless eat a diet of candy and dessert, if we let them have from the beginning only what they want. Many of them would doubtless learn to like narcotics or hard liquor at an early age, if we made those things readily available. . . . One of the responsibilities of adults is to guide the tastes and values of children as they develop. To say that television should give children whatever they want is a thoroughly irresponsible and callous point of view. (p. 180)

But we cannot depend upon the commercial networks as they now exist to take responsibility for appropriate children's programming. Thus, suggestions have been offered to retain the commercial system — but with a restructuring that might better lead to improved TV fare.

CHANGES IN FINANCING

Major complaints about television often revolve around the lack of innovation and experimentation, and the avoidance of controversial and/or intellectual topics. Critics point the finger of blame at the commercial structure of television. In their efforts to provide the most popular programs (and thus entice advertisers to spend their money), the networks tend to do what is safest — imitate the successful programs already on the air. This accounts for the cyclical nature of television — one successful medical, legal, or detective show spawns a host of hopeful copies. In precisely imitating each other, the networks have perpetuated violence and avoided the "danger" of innovations.

An obvious solution to the dilemma is to change the way television is financed. What is not so obvious is how to do it. Fairfax M. Cone, chairman of an advertising agency, suggests that advertisers continue to pay for programs, but with reduced choice—all advertisers pay for all programs[9]. As he would have it, the networks would:

> ... *revolve advertisers through the total week's programming; to cut out, as it were, preferred positions in the weekly schedule, and to open this up to experimentation, with every advertiser paying his share ... if [advertisers] hold to their preferred positions, which means positions in certain large-audience programs, their competitors must seek to equal them (they have no choice) and the level of television programming will remain precisely what it is — which is a national disgrace.* (p. 87)

Certainly, Cone's idea is well intentioned. However, it may not be sufficient, and could backfire. Currently the networks compete for audiences and advertising dollars, and programs within a network compete with each other. Cone's plan removes the latter type of competition but not the former, since advertisers would still select the network with which to do business. The networks, then, might attempt to make *every* program a high audience attraction, because they would have to sell their entire schedule. The plan, therefore, could result in poorer programming.

A second possibility for changing the financial system involves shifting the sources of monies from the advertiser to the viewer. One way of doing this might be some variant of the British system, in which each owner pays a tax on his set (buys a yearly license) which goes into a public, nongovernment controlled corporation that produces programs.

The broadcasting system in the Netherlands provides still another alternative to our present financing system[10]. Television licenses there are distributed by a government agency to broadcasting associations, who are forbidden *by law* from financing through commercial broadcasting. Commercials do appear on Dutch television (placed so as not to interfere with ongoing programs), but the time is sold by an independent government agency. Thus, the broadcasters are not directly responsible to the advertisers.

They are, on the other hand, responsible to viewers. Broadcasting associations must: (1) consist of a minimum of 100,000 members, (2) air a complete program schedule, including information, music, education, and so on, (3) have the ability to satisfy the needs of the community, and (4) be nonprofit making. On the surface, requirements (2) and (3) sound suspiciously like "requirements" for a license in the United States. However, the membership requirement and the lack of commercial control make it considerably more likely that the broadcast associations will meet the needs of the community.

Two other aspects of the Dutch system warrant our attention. The associations are allotted air time on a basis proportional to their memberships. A maximum of 10% of total broadcast time is available to specially licensed groups who cannot muster the required 100,000. Thus, the majorities dominate broadcasting—but the minorities are not forgotten. A second, related aspect of the system provides for quality. A potential problem in providing air time to minority groups is amateurish results, since they may not be able to afford the equipment involved in making professional programs. To prevent this, all equipment and other technical resources are pooled. The Dutch Broadcasting Foundation administers studios and electronic equipment, and employs technical personnel.

The Dutch system obviously cannot be transported unchanged to the United States, but it could be adapted. Jeff Greenfield has made some suggestions[11]. His plan includes paying a TV tax—Greenfield mentions $1 per month per set—to pay production costs. So far, that is not too different from the British system, recommended by the Carnegie Commission. The difference lies in determining who gets the money. Under the British system a public corporation allocates funds; under the Dutch system the tax payers vote directly on the producers who will receive support.

Thus, according to Greenfield's plan, anyone could run for producership: a political group, a sports association, a rock group promoter, or a symphony orchestra. All producers who received a certain minimum number of votes would get a proportional amount of air time—and the money needed to create their programs. The only constraint placed on producers, other than libel, would be the duty not to bore viewers. In this way, a heterogeneous selection of programs, necessarily true to public tastes, would be created.

DIRECT PRESSURES ON COMMERCIAL BROADCASTING

In many ways the most obvious, and perhaps most feasible, way of changing today's programming involves direct pressures on commercial broadcasting. The existing commercial system, with its enormous resources and potential, would thus be preserved. Two apparent means for accomplishing this goal are sanctions from the public and regulation by the federal government.

Regardless of which tack is taken, a principal concern of the commercial interests, in both ridding children's shows of violent content and producing better ones, is the fear of losing its audience. There is every indication that the fear is wholly unwarranted. In Chapter 2, we saw that violent shows are not uniquely preferred forms of entertainment; indeed, first-graders do not select any highly violent programs and show a strong affinity for *Sesame Street*. In addition, it has been shown that children spend as much time watching TV when all the available offerings on a given evening are judged mediocre as when all are judged highly appealing. Youngsters will, of course, choose among the alternatives. But what those alternatives are is controlled by the industry; changes involve only prudent control of availability. The observation is not a new one[8]:

> *When educational programs like "Science Review," "From Tropical Forests," or "Have You a Camera?" appeared on BBC, children who had access to both BBC and the commercial channel would almost invariably turn to the commercial one, where they would find usually a choice of cartoons, Westerns, and the like, much like American commercial television. But if the child had access only to BBC—that is, if the commercial service had not yet reached his community—then there was a choice only of turning off the set or of watching the educational program. Under those circumstances, the English investigators report, "quite a number of children chose to see such programmes* and in fact enjoyed them." (p. 95, emphasis in original)

Sanctions by Private Citizens

One important source of influence to change programming is through economic sanctions imposed on advertisers. Alberta Siegel, a member of the Surgeon General's Advisory Committee and former editor of the prominent professional journal, *Child Development*, has suggested[12]:

> ... that consumers convey their disapproval of violence vendors in two ways. We may refuse to purchase their products. And we may refuse to buy stock in their firms. *The purpose of commercial television is to sell products. If consumers boycott products that are*

*advertised on programs glorifying aggression and teaching tech-
niques of mayhem and massacre, perhaps the producers of these
products will turn their energies to finding other techniques of
attracting customers. Many investors today are guided in their
investing by social concerns. Churches, universities, foundations,
union pension plans, and others are seeking to invest their funds in
ways that benefit society. If these groups know who the violence
vendors are, they may withdraw investment funds from their firms
and instead invest their funds in those manufacturers who sponsor
wholesome entertainment for the next generation.* (p. 64, original
emphasis)

In the same vein, of course, citizens may reward sponsors who devote
their resources to improved children's programming. This can best be
accomplished by purchasing their products. Letters of commendation to
firms that show such initiative do not go unnoticed; when ACT elected to
praise a commercial program, it made headlines in *Broadcasting* magazine.

Increased Government Regulation

Broadcasters have long argued that government control over television
would be both illegal (violating the First Amendment of freedom of
speech) and unnecessary.

According to current legal interpretations of the First Amendment
broadcasters are indeed immune from federal control except:

1. if the materials presented are intrinsically injurious;
2. if the contents are dangerous to the state;
3. if the materials are of a purely private nature (e.g., advertisements).

Obscenity has usually been included under the concept of intrinsically
injurious, and the networks steer clear of controversy by themselves
censoring content which could be labeled obscene. But we have seen that
they do not effectively do so in regard to violence, for which there is
better evidence to support the label "injurious."

Vitalizing the FCC

At the same time, the FCC has proved largely ineffective as a regulatory body. At present, the powers of the FCC are sufficient to produce
some improvement, if the commission took its licensing task more serious-
ly. Its practices now are a mockery of the concept of serving the public

interest. But they can be changed. As early as 1960, Consumer's Union urged the FCC[6]:

> *Make hearings mandatory in all license renewals .... To obtain its highly prized license to operate—the right to use the public domain: an air channel—a TV or radio station vies with other contestants by, among other things, promising programs of quality. Every three years, according to law, a broadcasting license must be renewed. Although the FCC has the power to hold a renewal hearing to determine how well the licensee has carried out his promises, it has been most lax on this score. In 1958, for example, out of the 1500 or so radio and TV renewals granted, only two renewal hearings were held .... Hold all such renewal hearings, as well as new license hearings, in the locale of the broadcasting station, so that the community to be served may be heard.*
>
> *Since community tastes and interests may differ, local set-owners are, obviously, the ones best situated not only to know what they want over the air, but what the actual program content has been. It makes little sense, therefore, to hold license hearings in Washington, D.C., where attendance is limited, practically speaking, to the industry's lobbyists, attorneys, and public relations personnel. Publicize the renewal hearings over the stations involved for a given number of days at fixed hours, and invite public participation in the proceedings.*
>
> *A public hearing of which the public is unaware is hardly public.*
>
> *Require each broadcaster to maintain for public investigation the commitments he made with regard to programming and advertising when he was granted his license.*
>
> *The promises made by the broadcaster as a condition to his receipt of a license are not, practically speaking, a matter of public record unless access to such commitments is made easily available to the particular consumers whose sets receive the particular licensee's broadcasts.* (1960, pp. 109–110)

Consumers Union also suggested the formation of a Consumer's Council as an advisory body to the FCC. It would review licensing decisions, the performance of licensees, and publicize its findings. Crucial in each of these innovations would be some independent form of monitoring. Alberta Siegel has also noted the need for such an agency[12]:

> ... we need an independent monitoring agency to provide regular
> reports on the level of violence in television entertainment. This
> agency could issue periodic "smog bulletins," alerting the public
> to the level of violent pollution currently being emitted by their TV
> receivers. I suggest that this agency might be privately financed,
> by one of the foundations, and that reports should be issued at
> least monthly. These reports should be broadcast over television
> and should appear in newspapers and magazines .... They should
> indicate how much violence is occurring, which networks and
> stations are broadcasting it, the times it is being broadcast and
> how many child viewers are estimated to be watching at those
> times. They should also indicate who the sponsors are for the
> violent shows ... (pp. 63-66)

In addition to enforcing regulations already in effect, the FCC could be
given additional powers. On June 8, 1972, U.S. Congressman John M.
Murphy introduced a bill which provides for regulation of the *networks*
(not just the stations) through the FCC. Murphy, long an advocate of
improving children's television, included these remarks in his statement[13]:

> ... In introducing a bill for the regulation of the networks, I am
> fully aware that, in the last analysis, it is those who have been
> licensed by the Federal Communications Commission to operate
> the nation's television stations who must bear the ultimate respon-
> sibility for the violence and triviality that today dominate American
> television ....
>
> Past experience has shown that it will be a long time—perhaps
> never—before the TV broadcasters eliminate violence from TV.
> That is, unless there is a vigorous move by the government to force
> them to stop. But the members of the Senate Communications
> Committee themselves professed frustration when it came to
> recommending a solution to TV violence because of first amend-
> ment considerations .... Previous attempts at eliminating TV
> violence by relying on the "good faith" of the TV industry by
> several House and Senate Committees, the Federal Communica-
> tions Commission, and the President's Commission on Violence
> have been marked by failure. Failure because these groups all
> deplored violence on television; with varying degrees of sophistica-
> tion they pointed to TV violence as a negative influence on human

behavior; and, they were lulled into inaction with promises from the TV industry that there would be a diminishment of violence if the industry were allowed to "clean up its own house." And, as of May, 1972, the net result of all of this has been a lamentable cipher. Over and above the question of whether TV violence is harmful, the networks have, for the past 18 years, assiduously violated their own codes of ethics and standards of broadcasting. In the face of an 18 year history of failure at self control, I feel it is safe to conclude that we cannot depend on the TV industry to clean its own house of TV violence. They obviously will not . . . .

I have decided to introduce legislation to give the F.C.C. the authority to regulate the networks in the area of prime time programming. The recent anti-trust suits by the Justice Department would divest the networks of their production of these shows altogether. I am against such drastic action.

As I pointed out, given our system, the networks, and only the networks, have the capability to produce quality television on a sustained basis. We need them. My bill would not take this function away from them — it would only make them produce programs more in the public interest.

Murphy's bill, HR 15408, would grant the FCC power to enumerate specific rules and regulations and to fine the networks for noncompliance.

The case against TV's present offerings is clear. But we cannot eliminate the medium's impact on the lives of our children, even if we wished to do so. Children, we now know, will learn from television entertainment regardless of a program's content — or purpose. As FCC Commissioner Nicholas Johnson astutely observed: "All television is educational television. The only question is, what is it teaching?"

The medium, we have seen, is a powerful force which operates through observational learning, itself a natural process which is continually at work in the lives of our children. Thus, technology has given us a uniquely potent teacher — and in a complex society like our own, effective teachers are much needed. At the same time, though, the greater the power of the teacher, the greater is its capacity to work for either good or harm. It behooves us, in a world on the brink of disaster, to harness televison's potential to contribute to our society in ways which we deem more desirable.

All of us must bear the responsibility for what is being taught on television. Accepting it squarely can lead to programming which serves the highest values of society—a medium which is truly in the public interest. In the past, children have seen and learned violence on TV's window and today they continue to do so. In the future they might, instead, learn constructive solutions to the problems they will face. Which will it be? The choice is ours.

REFERENCES

1. Fleiss, D. & Ambrosino, L. *An international comparison of children's television programming.* Washington, D.C.: National Citizens Committee for Broadcasting, 1971.
2. The Carnegie Commission. *Public Television: A program for action.* New York: Harper & Row, 1967.
3. Henry, E. W. *Remarks before the International Radio and Television Society.* Speech delivered on October 2, 1964. Reprinted in H. J. Skornia and J. W. Kitson (eds.). *Problems and controversies in television and radio.* Palo Alto, California: Pacific Books, 1968.
4. Mayer, M. *About television.* New York: Harper & Row, 1972.
5. Minow, N. N. *Equal time: The private broadcaster and the public interest.* New York: Atheneum, 1964. (Copyright © 1964 by Newton N. Minow. Reprinted by permission of Atheneum Publishers.)
6. Here, we would suggest, is a program for the FCC. *Consumer Reports*, February 1960. (Copyright © Consumers Union.)
7. Friendly, F. W. *Due to circumstances beyond our control.* New York: Random House, 1967. (Copyright © 1967 by Fred W. Friendly. Reprinted by permission of Random House, Inc.)
8. Schramm, W., Lyle, J., & Parker, E. B. *Television in the lives of our children.* Stanford, California: Stanford University Press, 1961.
9. Cone, F. M. *The two publics of television.* Paper presented to the Broadcasting Advertising Club of Chicago, Chicago, Illinois, October, 1961. Reprinted in H. J. Skornia and J. W. Kitson (eds.). *Problems and controversies in television and radio.* Palo Alto, California: Pacific Books, 1968.
10. Schaafsma, H. Mirror of a pillarized society: Broadcasting in the Netherlands. *Delta, A Review of Arts, Life and Thought in the Netherlands*, 1967, 9.
11. Greenfield, J. TV belongs to us. *Newsday*, July 30, 1972.
12. U.S. Congress, Senate. Hearings before the Subcommittee on Communications of the Commerce Committee, March 1972.
13. Murphy, J. M. Statement of Representative John M. Murphy on the introduction of a bill to regulate the television networks. June 8, 1972.

APPENDIX A

The list that follows* describes each of the research reports and related publications of the NIMH Surgeon General's inquiry. The papers themselves are available in seven volumes:

Television and Social Behavior: Media Content and Control (Reports and Papers, Volume 1)

Television and Social Behavior: Television and Social Learning (Reports and Papers, Volume 2)

Television and Social Behavior: Television and Adolescent Aggressiveness (Reports and Papers, Volume 3)

Television and Social Behavior: Television in Day-to-Day Life: Patterns of Use (Reports and Papers, Volume 4)

Television and Social Behavior: Television's Effects: Further Explorations (Reports and Papers, Volume 5)

Television and Growing Up: The Impact of Televised Violence (Report of the Surgeon General's Scientific Advisory Committee on Television and Social Behavior)

Television and Social Behavior: An Annotated Bibliography of Research Focusing on Television's Impact on Children

*Reprinted, with minor modifications, from *Television and Growing Up: The Impact of Televised Violence.*

Any of these volumes can be purchased from the Superintendent of
Documents, U.S. Government Printing Office, Washington, D.C. 20402

Author and Title	Subjects	Description

1. Baldwin & Lewis
    Violence in Television:
    The Industry Looks at
    Itself
    (Volume 1)
	48 producers,
	writers, and
	directors
		Interviews were conducted with the
		writers, producers, and directors of
		network action-adventure program-
		ming. The respondents were asked
		to describe the role of violence in
		such programs and how the indus-
		try handles this aspect (i.e., censor-
		ship activities). In addition, the
		subjects were asked to respond to
		the critics of television violence
		and to comment on their beliefs
		about the possible effects of view-
		ing televised violence.

2. Bechtel, Achelpohl, &
    Akers
    Correlates between
    Observed Behavior and
    Questionnaire Responses
    on Television Viewing
    (Volume 4)
	20 families
	Total $N = 82$
		Video tape cameras were installed in
		the homes of participating families.
		Observations of viewing behavior
		were continuously recorded for five
		days. The video tape records were
		coded, in $2\frac{1}{2}$ minute intervals for
		attention to the set (e.g., watching/
		not watching), and types of simul-
		taneous activity (e.g., eating, read-
		ing). These behavior records were
		compared with the viewer's
		responses to questionnaire
		measures of viewing behavior.

3. Blatt, Spencer, & Ward
    A Cognitive Develop-
    mental Study of
    Children's Reactions to
    Television Advertising
    (Volume 4)
	20 children
	5 kindergarten
	5 second grade
	5 fourth grade
	5 sixth grade
		Children were shown a one-hour
		videotape of "Saturday morning"
		television programming which
		included cartoons and other chil-
		dren's programs, plus 15 minutes
		of commercials. On the following
		day, the children were interviewed,
		in groups of five, concerning their
		reactions to the commercials (e.g.,
		recall and understanding of the
		commercial message) and general
		attitudes toward advertising.

4. Cantor
    The Role of the
    Producer in Choosing
	24 producers and
	writers
		Twenty producers and four writers of
		children's programs were inter-
		viewed. Respondents were asked

Author and Title	Subjects	Description
Children's Television Content (Volume 1)		to describe the manner in which shows are selected by the networks and sponsors; the relationship between the producers and network; and the producer's conception of the audience for his program.
5. Chaffee Television and Adolescent Aggressiveness (Volume 3)		A summary of current research on the relationship between viewing televised violence and the aggressive behavior of adolescents.
6. Chaffee & McLeod Adolescent Television Use in the Family Context (Volume 3)	1292 junior and senior high school 641 eighth grade 651 tenth grade	This survey related adolescent's television viewing (e.g., viewing televised violence) to factors such as; IQ, parent's television use, SES, and family communication patterns. The latter factor was defined by the parent's relative emphasis on either socio — (i.e., maintaining interpersonal harmony/repression of conflicts) or concept — (i.e., free discussion and mutual understanding of conflicts) orientations.
7. Clark Race Identification, and Television Violence Experiment I (Volume 5)	71 teenagers 38 white 33 black	Adolescents were shown a videotape of a Dragnet episode which featured three main characters: "Black Militant," "Black Policeman," and "White Policeman." The subjects viewed the program in either racially "mixed" or "homogeneous" groups. Postviewing questionnaires assessed the viewer's identification with the various characters and the role of black consciousness in such identification.
Experiment II (Volume 5)	45 white, college students	Subjects viewed the Dragnet program in dyads composed of either a black or white confederate who either engaged in social communication (i.e., friendly conversation) or remained silent during the viewing period.

Author and Title	Subjects	Description
8. Clark & Blankenburg Trends in Violent Content in Selected Mass Media (Volume 1)		Several forms of mass media (e.g., front page newspaper stories, a weekly magazine, and television entertainment programming) were inspected for the presence of violent content and their treatment of violent themes. Comparisons were obtained between media violence and environmental or real violence (i.e., FBI Uniform Crime Reports).
9. Comstock Media Control and Content: An Overview (Volume 1)		A review of this program's research on decision-making in television production and violence in television content.
10. Dahlgren Television in the Sociali- zation Process: Structures and Programming of the Swedish Broadcasting Corporation (Volume 1)		A description of the broadcast policies of Sveriges Radio.
11. Dominick & Greenberg Attitudes Toward Vio- lence: The Interaction of TV Exposure, Family Attitudes, and Social Class (Volume 3)	838 children 434, fourth-, fifth-, and sixth-grade boys 404, fourth-, fifth-, and sixth-grade girls	Each child's prior exposure to televised violence, his perception of his parents' attitudes concerning the appropriateness of violence, and his family's socioeconomic level were related to various measures of the child's attitudes toward violence (e.g., willingness to use violence, perceived effectiveness of violence, and approval of aggression).
12. Ekman, Liebert, Friesen, Harrison, Zlatchin, Malmstrom, & Baron Facial Expressions of Emotion While Watching Televised Violence as Predictors of Subsequent Aggression (Volume 5)	65, 5–6-year-old children (30 boys and 35 girls)	Children's facial expression while viewing televised violence were used as an index of the child's emotional reaction to such fare. This index was then used to assess the relationship between the child's emotional response to observing violent acts and his subsequent willingness to engage in interpersonal aggression.

Author and Title	Subjects	Description
13. Feshbach Reality and Fantasy in Filmed Violence Experiment I (Volume 2)	129, 9–11-year-old children	Children viewed either real (i.e., newsreel), fantasy (i.e., Hollywood movie), or control (e.g., circus movie) films and were then allowed to play a game in which they could engage in aggressive acts against an ostensible victim.
Experiment II (Volume 2)	40, 9–11-year-old children	In this study, each child was informed that the movie he was about to view was either real ("NBC news-reel") or fantasy ("Hollywood movie"). Measures of the child's subsequent aggressive behavior were identical to the first study.
Experiment III (Volume 2)	30, 9–11-year-old children	This study was similar to the second except that each child was informed that his aggressive behavior in the "guessing game" was only make believe. Results of this study were compared with the results of the previous experiment.
14. Feshbach & Singer Television and Aggression: Some Reactions to the Liebert, Sobol, and Davidson Review and Response (Volume 5)		A response to a comment on a reply to a critique of the catharsis thesis (*see* items 14, 35, and 36).
15. Feshbach & Singer Television and Aggression: A Reply to Liebert, Sobol, and Davidson. (Volume 5)		A reply to a critique of the catharsis thesis (*see* items 15, 35, and 36).
16. Foulkes, Belvedere, & Brubaker Televised Violence and Dream Content (Volume 5)	40, 10–12-year-old boys	This study was designed to assess the relationship between viewing televised violence and the subsequent content of the child's dreams. Children viewed either a violent or nonviolent program immediately prior to bedtime. Their dreams were monitored during the sleep period and scored on a variety of dimensions (e.g., hostility, vividness, and hedonic tone).

Author and Title	Subjects	Description
17. Friedman & Johnson Mass Media Use and Aggression: A Pilot Study (Volume 3)	80 preadolescent boys 40 "aggressive" 40 "nonaggres- sive"	Adolescent's attitudes toward aggression (e.g., tendency to engage in overt physical aggression) and his patterns of television use (e.g., amount of time spent viewing, program preferences) were studied in an attempt to assess the relationship between viewing televised violence and engaging in antisocial acts.
18. Gerbner The Structure and Process of Television Program Content Regulation in the United States (Volume 1)		A description of broadcast and content control structures operative in American television programming.
19. Gerbner Violence in Television Drama: Trends and Symbolic Functions (Volume 1)		This study provided an analysis of a one week sample of prime time entertainment programming. It described various factors relating to the frequency and symbolic characteristics of televised violence.
20. Greenberg Television's Effects: Further Explorations (Volume 5)		An overview of several current research projects that provide a diversity of theoretical and methodological approaches to research on the effects of television.
21. Greenberg, Ericson, & Vlahos Children's Television Behaviors as Perceived by Mother and Child (Volume 4)	85, fourth- and fifth- grade children and their mothers	Mothers, interviewed at home, were asked to describe their child's viewing patterns (e.g., program preferences, rules about viewing) while each child answered similar questions in the classroom. The child's self reported viewing behavior was compared with the mother's description.
22. Greenberg & Gordon Perceptions of Violence in Television Programs: Critics and the Public (Volume 1)	53 critics 303 men and women	A telephone survey (public) and mail questionnaires (critics) asked the respondents to rate the amount of violence contained in various television entertainment programs.

Title	Subjects	Description
...enberg & Gordon Social Class and Racial Differences in Children's Perception of Televised Violence (Volume 5)	325 fifth-grade boys 89 low SES white 89 low SES black 90 middle SES white 57 upper SES white	This study assessed boys' evaluation of violence portrayed on television in terms of the degree of perceived violence, acceptibility of violence, liking, degree of arousal, and perceived reality of the violent act.
24. Greenberg & Gordon Children's Perceptions of Television Violence: A Replication (Volume 5)	263 eighth-grade boys 66 low SES black 78 low SES white 37 middle SES white 82 upper-middle SES white.	A replication of the prior study conducted with younger boys (*see* item 23).
25. Gurevitch The Structure and Content of Television Broadcasting in Four Countries: An Overview (Volume 1)		An introduction to a review of the broadcasting policies of Great Britain, Israel, Sweden, and the United States.
26. Halloran & Croll Television Programmes in Great Britain: Content and Control (Volume 1)		A discussion of television broadcasting in Great Britain.
27. Israel & Robinson Demographic Characteristics of Viewers of Television Violence and News Programs (Volume 4)	6834 adults	Information on preferences and viewing patterns of a nationwide survey of adult television viewers were related to various demographic characteristics (e.g., age, education, income, sex).
28. Johnson, Friedman, & Gross Four Masculine Styles in Television Programming: A Study of the Viewing Preferences of	80, eighth-grade boys 39 "aggressive" 41 "nonaggressive"	This study compared the program preference patterns of boys with a history of "social aggressiveness" with their nonaggressive peers in an attempt to construct a program classification scheme based on the

Author and Title	Subjects	Description
Adolescent Males (Volume 3)		masculine role concept portrayed in each program.
29. Katzman Violence and Color Television: What Children of Different Ages Learn (Volume 5)	240, fourth-, sixth-, and ninth-grade boys	Children viewed (in either color or black-and-white format) a color television program which had been edited into either "high-violence" or "low-violence" versions. Post-viewing measures tested the child's recall of central and peripheral details and related this recall to the color/violence variations.
30. Kenny Threats to the Internal Validity of Cross-Lagged Panel Inference, as re-lated to "Television Violence and Child Aggression: A Follow-up Study" (Volume 3)		A methodological note on the research design employed in a study by Lefkowitz, Eron, Walder, & Huesmann (see item 31).
31. Lefkowitz, Eron, Walder, & Huesmann Television Violence and Child Aggression: A Follow-up Study (Volume 3)	875 children— third-grade sample 382 adolescent eighth-grade sample 427, 19-year-olds	As part of a longitudinal study of childhood aggression, the investi-gators queried the child and/or his parents about his television view-ing patterns (e.g., program prefer-ences). Cross-lagged correlations between television viewing at age three and adolescent aggressive-ness at age 19 were obtained to provide causal inferences regarding television's role in the develop-ment of aggressive behavior.
32. Leifer & Roberts Children's Responses to Television Violence Experiment I (Volume 2)	271 children 40 kindergarten 54 third grade 56 sixth grade 51 ninth grade 70 twelfth grade	Subsequent to viewing a television program which contained a number of violent acts each child was asked to evaluate the motivations and consequences surrounding each depicted act of violence. The child's understanding of these characteristics of violent act was then assessed in terms of the child's willingness to engage in aggressive behavior.

Author and Title	Subjects	Description
Experiment II (Volume 2)	132 children 62 preschool 40 fifth grade 30 twelfth grade	Each child viewed a television program which was edited to provide one of four combinations of motivations/consequences for the portrayed violent acts: good-good, good-bad, bad-good, bad-bad. Post-viewing measures were similar to the prior study.
Experiment III (Volume 2)	160 children 51 fourth grade 56 seventh grade 53 tenth grade	Children viewed one of two versions of a movie in which the justifications for aggression had been edited to provide for an "aggression-less justified" version. Post-viewing measures of aggressive behavior were similar to those employed in the first experiment.
Experiment IV (Volume 2)	349 children 99 third grade 138 sixth grade 112 tenth grade	The temporal separation of the motivations for an aggressive act and consequences accruing to the aggressor on the child's post-viewing aggressive behavior, was explored in this present study. Measures of aggressive behavior were similar to previous studies.
33. Liebert Some Relationships Between Viewing Violence and Behaving Aggressively (Volume 2)		A review of current research on television's role in the imitation and/or disinhibition of aggressive behavior (with an additional report: Strauss & Poulos, "Television and Social Learning: A summary of the Experimental Effects of Observed Filmed Aggression").
34. Liebert & Baron Short-Term Effects of Televised Aggression on Children's Aggressive Behavior (Volume 2)	136 children (68 boys and 68 girls) (65, 5–6-year-olds) (71, 8–9-year-olds)	In this study the child-viewer's willingness to engage in interpersonal aggression was assessed subsequent to viewing either aggressive or neutral television programming.
35. Liebert, Davidson, & Sobol Catharsis of Aggression Among Institutionalized		A comment on a reply to a critique of the catharsis thesis (*see* item 14, 15, and 36).

Author and Title	Subjects	Description
Boys: Further Comments (Volume 5)		
36. Liebert, Sobol, & Davidson Catharsis of Aggression Among Institutionalized Boys: Fact or Artifact? (Volume 5)		A commentary on a study of the role of catharsis in evaluating the effects of viewing televised violence (*see* items 14, 15, and 35).
37. LoSciuto A National Inventory of Television Viewing Behavior (Volume 4)	252 families	A nationwide sample of American families were interviewed concerning various aspects of television viewing such as: why people watch television, what they learn from programs, extent of viewing, and program preferences
38. Lyle Television in Day-to-Day Life: Patterns of Use (Volume 4)		A review of current research on the role of television in some aspects of daily life.
39. Lyle & Hoffman Children's Use of Television and Other Media (Volume 4)	1682 children 300 first grade 793–877, sixth grade 469–505, tenth grade	Children were interviewed about the role television plays in their daily life (e.g., extent and duration of viewing, program preferences, attitudes toward television, use of other forms of mass media). In addition, the mothers of first-graders were also interviewed concerning their perceptions of the role of television viewing patterns and perceived extent of learning from television.
40. Lyle & Hoffman Explorations in patterns of television viewing by preschool children (Volume 4)	158 children 40 3-year-olds 82 4-year-olds 35 5-year-olds 1 6-year-old	A selected sample of Caucasian, Negro and Mexican–American preschool boys and girls were interviewed concerning their television viewing (e.g., program preferences, extent of viewing recognition of television characters). In addition, mothers were interviewed concerning their child's television viewing patterns and perceived extent of learning from television.

Author and Title	Subjects	Description
41. McIntyre & Teevan Television and Deviant Behavior (Volume 3)	2270 junior and senior high school students	Questionnaire responses were used to provide an estimate of the relationship between television viewing patterns (e.g., program preferences) and self reported aggressive and delinquent behavior.
42. McLeod, Atkin, & Chaffee Adolescents, Parents and Television Use: Self-Report and Other- Report Measures from the Wisconsin Sample (Volume 3)	648 students Maryland sample 229, seventh grade 244, tenth grade Wisconsin sample 68, seventh grade 83, tenth grade	Self-report, peer, and "other" rated indices of aggressive behavior were related to various aspects of the adolescent's pattern of television use (e.g., extent of viewing, pro- gram preferences, cognitive reac- tions to televised violence).
43. McLeod, Atkin, & Chaffee Adolescents, Parents and Television Use: Adoles- cent Self-Report and Other-Report Measures from the Maryland and Wisconsin Sample (Volume 3)		*See* item 42: A comparison between adolescent television viewing and self reported aggressive or delin- quent behavior.
44. Murray Television in Inner- City Homes: Viewing Behavior of Young Boys (Volume 4)	27, 5–6-year-old boys	Observation of in-home television viewing, parent–child interviews, diary records of one week's tele- vision viewing and measures of cognitive and social development were used to provide a description of the role television plays in the daily lives of a selected sample of young boys (with an additional report: Furfey, "First Graders Watching Television").
45. Neale Comment on: Television Violence and Child Aggression: A Follow- up Study (Volume 3)		A methodological note on the Lefkowitz, Eron, Walder, & Huesmann study (*see* item 31).
46. Rabinovitch, MacLean, Markham, & Talbott Children's Violence	57 sixth-grade children 24 girls	This study was designed to assess changes in the child's perception of violence as a result of viewing

Author and Title	Subjects	Description
Perception as a Function of Television Violence (Volume 5)	33 boys	televised violence. Children viewed either an aggressive or nonaggressive television program and were then presented with a discrimination task (i.e., identifying a tachistoscopically presented slide as either "violent" or "nonviolent").
47. Robinson Television's Impact on Everyday Life: Some Cross-National Evidence (Volume 4)		This study was focused on the respondent's allocation of time ("time-budgets") to various activities (e.g., work, child care, leisure, mass media use) in his daily life. Time budgets were sampled in 15 cities in 11 counties.
48. Robinson Toward Defining the Functions of Television (Volume 4)		A review of current research on the role of television in relation to other daily activities.
49. Robinson & Bachman Television Viewing Habits and Aggression (Volume 3)	1559, 19-year-old males	As part of a nationwide survey of the changing characteristics of youth, respondents were asked to indicate the extent of their television viewing, program preferences, and the locus of "greatest-learning-about-life" – television vs. school. These findings were then related to the respondents' self-reported incidence of aggressive and delinquent behaviors.
50. Shinar Structure and Content of Television Broadcasting in Israel (Volume 1)		A review of television broadcasting policies in Israel.
51. Stein & Friedrich Television Content and Young Children's Behavior (Volume 2) (with Vondracek)	97, $3\frac{1}{2}$–$5\frac{1}{2}$-year-olds 52 boys 45 girls	Preschool children were exposed to either an "aggressive, neutral, or prosocial" television diet and then observed during the course of their daily interaction with other children in their classroom. The observations were conducted over a nine-week period including three-week baseline, four-week

Author and Title	Subjects	Description
		controlled viewing, and two-week follow-up periods. Changes (over baseline) in either aggressive or prosocial behaviors were used to provide a measure of the impact of television programming.
52. Stevenson Television and the Behavior of Preschool Children (Volume 2)		A discussion of research findings on the impact of television in early childhood and suggestions for future research.
53. Tannenbaum Studies in Film- and TV-Mediated Arousal and Aggression (Volume 5)		A review of research and theory on mediating factors (e.g., emotional arousal) in the relationships between viewing televised violence and subsequent aggressive behavior.
54. Wackman, Reale. & Ward Racial Differences in Responses to Advertising Among Adolescents (Volume 4)	1149, eighth–twelfth-grade 1049 whites 100 blacks	This study was focused on a comparison of the responses of black-and-white adolescents to television advertising in terms of their favorite ads, extent of "learning consumer roles," and reasons offered for viewing commercials.
55. Ward Effects of Television Advertising on Children and Adolescents (Volume 4)		A review and discussion of research, in the current program, on the impact of television advertising.
56. Ward, Levinson, & Wackman Children's Attention to Television Advertising (Volume 4)	134 mothers of 5–12-year-old children	Interviews were conducted with the mothers of young children in order to determine the short-term consequences of watching television advertising.
57. Ward, Reale. & Levinson Children's Perceptions, Explanations, and Judgments of Television Advertising: A Further Exploration. (Volume 4)		An elaboration of the Blatt, Spencer, & Ward study (*see* item 3).

Author and Title	Subjects	Description
58. Ward & Robertson Adolescent Attitudes Toward Television Advertising (Volume 4)	1094, eighth– twelfth-grade	This study was designed to relate adolescent's attitudes toward tele- vision advertising to demographic characteristics, family communica- tion patterns, and television use.
59. Ward & Wackman Family and Media Influences on Adoles- cent Consumer Learning (Volume 4)	1094, eighth– twelfth-grade	This survey assessed the adolescent's "consumer skills" (i.e., recall of advertising content, attitudes toward commercials, materialistic attitudes, and buying behavior) and related these skills to various demographic characteristics.
60. Ward & Wackman Television Advertising and Intra-Family Influence: Children's Purchase Influence Attempts and Parental Yielding (Volume 4)	109 mothers of 5–12-year-old children	Interviewers asked the mothers of young children to describe the "effects of television advertising" in terms of the frequency and inten- sity of their child's "requests" for advertised products

INDEX*

Achelpohl, C., 116–117, *131*, *173*
Action for Children's Television, 122–126, *132*
Advertising, 111–132, 136–140, 163–164
  attention, 117, 127–128
  children's commercials, 121–126
  cigarette commercials, 136–138
  class action suit, 139–140
  content of commercials, 118–119
  counter-advertisement, 139–140
  fraudulent and deceptive advertising, 125–126, 138–140
  frequency of commercials, 117–118
  influence on programming, 119–121
  reactions to commercials, 128–131
  revenues, 111–115
  stereotypes in commercials, 118–119
  toy advertising, 124–126
  vitamin commercials, 122–124
Age
  perception of reality, 30
  reactions to advertising, 127–131
  viewing time, 9–10
Aggressive behavior, aggressive play, 41–42, 52, 53–58
  behavior observation, 83, 86

behavior rating scale, 46–48, 71
  definition of aggression, 52–53
  fantasy aggression, 52
  peer ratings, 81–82
  physical discomfort, 59–62
  response hierarchy, 62–66
  self-report, 72, 73–74, 74–75, 76–77
Akers, R., 116–117, *131*, *173*
Albert, R., 10, *13*
Ambrosino, L., 112–114, 158–159, *131*, *171*
American Broadcasting Corporation, 124, 136, 141–142, 146–148, 150, 154
Applefield, J. M., 83–85, *88*
Arlen, M. J., 28, *32*
Atkin, C. K., 9, 31, 76–80, *13*, *32*, *87*, *182*
Aubrey, J. T., 147

Bachman, J. G., 74–75, *87*, *183*
Baker, R. K., 23, 140–149, *32*, *156*
Baldwin, T. F., 15–18, 29, *31*, *173*
Ball, S., 99, 101, 103–108, *110*
Ball, S. J., 23, 140–149, *32*, *156*
Bandura, A., 39, 40, 41–43, 53–55, 58, 111–112, 150, *49*, *66*, *67*, *109*
Banzhaf, J., III, 136–138

*Full references are denoted by italic numerals.

187

Watson, A. S., 48, 149, *50*, *156*
Wells, W. D., 47–48, *50*
Wenham, B., 28, *32*
Wertham, F., 34–35, *48*
West, S., 48, *50*
White, G. M., 39, *49*
Whiteside, T., 136–138, *155*

Wiebe, G. O., 48, 149, 151–152, *50*, *156*
Willows, D. C., 58, *67*
Witty, P. A., 9, 89, *13*, *109*
Wolf, B. M., 52, 59, *66*
Wolf, T. M., 91, *109*

Zlatchin, C., *175*

TITLES IN THE PERGAMON GENERAL PSYCHOLOGY SERIES

CHILD BEHAVIOR MODIFICATION: A MANUAL FOR TEACHERS, NURSES, AND PARENTS

Pergamon General Psychology Series, Volume 24
By Luke S. Watson, Jr., Columbus State Institute, Columbus, Ohio

Written in laymen's language, this book is designed to teach principles of behavior modification based on the operant conditioning approach to teachers, occupational therapists, nurses, psychiatric aides, parents, and other para-professionals who work with mentally retarded, psychotic, and emotionally disturbed children. It provides sufficient information to deal with all problems that such persons encounter with children of this type in educational, institutional, and home settings. Testing materials are included to assure that the reader understands the essential points of the book.

**ADAPTIVE LEARNING: BEHAVIOR
MODIFICATION WITH CHILDREN**
Pergamon General Psychology Series, Volume 29
By B.A. Ashem and E.G. Poser

One of the few publications bringing together the major contributions so far made to the rapidly growing literature on behavior modification with children. It deals not only with techniques used in
modifying deviant behaviors such as occur in emotionally disturbed
and psychotic children, but also includes a chapter on the modification of behavior within the normal range. The final chapter demonstrates the wide variety of persons who can be helpful in bringing
about therapeutic behavior change in children.

SURVIVAL: BLACK/WHITE
Pergamon General Psychology Series, Volume 15
By Florence Halpern

Seeks to explain how the black people's struggle for survival has determined their particular way of perceiving and responding to their world. It is from this vantage point that the child-rearing practices, the concept of reality, the intellectual and educational problems of the black community must be understood. Such appreciation is essential if there is ever to be a meaningful coming together of the two races.